Trust and Obey!

(or how to become an evangelical Christian
and survive relatively unscathed)

by

Neil Bennett

authorHOUSE®

AuthorHouse™ UK Ltd.
500 Avebury Boulevard
Central Milton Keynes, MK9 2BE
www.authorhouse.co.uk
Phone: 08001974150

First published by AuthorHouse 10/17/2007

ISBN: 978-1-4343-3135-9 (sc)

Printed in the United States of America
Bloomington, Indiana
This book is printed on acid-free paper.

This book is a work of non-fiction. Unless otherwise noted, the author
and the publisher make no explicit guarantees as to the accuracy of
the information contained in this book and in some cases, names of
people and places have been altered to protect their privacy.

"I can't bear the religious labelling of children. Like four-year-old Islamic children or four-year-old Catholic children... If anything makes me see red, that does, because these children are too young to know what they are... Would you ever talk about a four-year-old neo-Keynesian monetarist? Or a four-year-old Gramscian Marxist? Of course you wouldn't. Religion is the one place where opinions about society, about philosophy, about cosmology are grafted on to labels tied round the necks of children."

(Richard Dawkins)

Dedicated to my Father without whose striving to give me a Christian upbringing I would not have had any material to write this book.

Note: The names of most of the persons portrayed in this book have been changed.

Contents

Prologue

This is a story about honesty – the honesty to look things in the face and say that they are as they are, and the intellectual honesty to admit when you just don't know. The Church will tell you that believing something for which you have insufficient evidence is a positive thing. The Bible, in Hebrews 11, verses 1 and 2, makes it clear: "*¹Now faith is being sure of what we hope for and certain of what we do not see. ²This is what the ancients were commended for...*". It is *commendable*, in other words, to mix up hope and knowledge, to "be sure" of what you hope for and "certain" about something unseen or for which there is no evidence. Conversely, lacking certainty about things unseen, being unsure about whether or not your hopes are going to be fulfilled, classifying beliefs and knowledge according to the amount of evidence you have to back them up smacks of cowardice and lack of resolution.

It may say so in the Epistle to the Hebrews, but this is dangerous nonsense. Wilfully giving your intellect the day off, believing in things unseen and being sure of what you hope for, whatever the evidence to the contrary, is the best way to render yourself defenceless against every passing charlatan. The hymn "Fight the Good Fight" may well be a rousing Victorian eulogy to the stiff upper lip, but its claim that "Only believe and thou shalt see..." is manifestly the wrong way round. Study the evidence and the counter-evidence, make a reasoned decision and *only then* believe would make a better mantra (although, regrettably, it wouldn't scan with the music).

At its most benign, the "only-believe-and-thou-shalt-see" mentality leads to an unhealthy interest in New Age mumbo-jumbo, belief in crystals, horoscopes, energy fields and rebirthing. At its most dangerous, it is the necessary seed-bed for fascism and can lead to irrational anger and violence. At the time of writing, mobs of young men throughout the Middle East are setting fire to Danish embassies and consular offices to protest against the publication of cartoon depictions of Mohammed in the Danish press. If these young men (and the young men who blew themselves up on the London Underground in July 2005, and the 9/11 hijackers in the United States) had been less "sure of what [they] hope for and certain of what [they] do not see", perhaps the start of the third millennium would have seen less disastrous relations between the post-Christian West and the Islamic World.

As German poet and Holocaust survivor Erich Fried eloquently put it:

" *Zweifle nicht an dem, der dir sagt, er hat Angst. Aber hab Angst vor dem, der dir sagt, er kennt keinen Zweifel.*"

["Doubt not the man who says he is afraid, but be afraid of the man who says that he has no doubts"].

Disinterest

Shadrach, Meshach, and Abednego escaping from the fiery furnace was one of the more lurid illustrations in my Children's Bible. I can still recall, with a frisson of horror, the vivid picture of the three friends engulfed in flames, "walking in the midst of the fire". My "Book of Children's Bible Stories" did not stint when it came it lurid pictures, designed to impress impressionable young minds, and some of the illustrations to the more fantastical parts of the Book of Revelations were fairly graphic, but somehow this picture of Daniel's companions subjected to an infernal ordeal is the one that has been engraved on my memory.

As my mother had looked after me during the day while my father was at work, he took over in the evenings, supervising my changing into pyjamas and teeth-brushing and then sweeping me onto his shoulders and, as he carried me upstairs to my room, pretending that he was a rocket and I was an astronaut being launched into orbit. I was fiercely proud of having been named 'Neil' after Neil Armstrong, who had taken his 'giant leap for mankind' in July of 1969 watched live by my mother, at that point four months pregnant with me, so the astronaut game was a clever invention by my father to ease my passage to bed. But, before I went to sleep, I was allowed two bedtime stories: one secular story and one Bible story. A traditional fairytale like Little Red Riding Hood, Snow White or my favourite, The 500 Hats of Bartholomew Cubbins by Dr Seuss, would be followed by Jonah and the Whale, the Israelites crossing the parted Red Sea or Saint John's description of the New Jerusalem.

As a four-year-old, I had little concept of how to interpret these stories. That the fairy tales were universally acknowledged as fiction but the Bible stories were considered by fundamentalists to be the literal truth, by some sceptics to be totally fictional or by liberal scholars to be somewhere in between was a concept far too sophisticated for me, so Abednego's fiery furnace, Jesus' miracles, Adam and Eve, the Seven Dwarfs and Goldilocks' deep dark forest occupied the same space in my imagination. Later on, when I started school and learnt to write, my childish prose reflected the highly imaginative part secular, part religious inner life I had started to develop. "I wish that I could have a vision and see all the people who have died and all the people in the Bible in Heaven," I once wrote as part of my Monday morning news. My teacher, a young woman not long out of college, was nonplussed at this precociousness, reflecting, I imagine, the description of the "New Jerusalem" in the Book of Revelation that my father had read from my "Children's Book of Bible Stories" the previous evening.

I grew up in a religious family. Not as religious as some – I know of families that went to church three times on a Sunday, a day on which television and playing outside were banned – but religious enough to mark us out as different in the secular 1970s. According to my parents, I was first taken to church as a tender babe-in-arms at the age of two weeks, and hardly missed a Sunday service from that point onwards until I was in my early twenties.

My father had a rather quaint idea of how things should be done in a Christian family. When I was a young child, we would meet around the fireplace in the living room for communal family prayers in the evenings before I went to bed. We would pray for all our relatives by name ("Please bless Grandma and Grandpa, Uncle Fred and Aunty Mary, and..."). These prayers soon fell victim to other demands on my parents' time and energy when my younger brother was born, but grace before meals, hymn-singing and Sunday church services punctuated my young life with unceasing regularity. My father's background was Baptist: he had attended his local Baptist church in his teens and was already a committed Christian when he joined the army as an older teenager. Motivated by Dr Billy Graham's London crusades in the mid 1950s, he went to Bible college and then trained as a religious education teacher. His evangelical, free-church background contrasted with my mother's more reserved, traditional Anglican background – her mother was for decades the organist of the parish church located just a stone's throw from the family home, and her brothers, my uncles, still complain today about having been made to sing in the church choir three times on a Sunday.

My parents, my brother and I attended the town's central Baptist church, in the days before worshippers would even have dreamed of clapping their hands, waving their arms in the air or 'speaking in tongues'. Electric guitars and drums had yet to make their appearance in churches and, as the musical instruments of choice for rock 'n' roll and other forms of popular music, were still considered to be slightly suspect (presumably, as they were held to lead to lascivious dancing and lewd thoughts), so the hymn singing would be accompanied by a thunderous organ whose pipes took up the entire front of the main church hall behind the elevated pulpit.

Every Sunday morning, the 'Sunday scramble', as my mother had christened it, began shortly after eight o'clock, with a roast joint of meat to be prepared and vegetables to be chopped for Sunday lunch (the most important meal of the week), hair to be combed and shoes to be polished. Attired in our Sunday best (this being the 1970s, this comprised enormously flared trousers, highly patterned shirts with long, pointed collars and a broad 'kipper' tie), feet squeezed into unyielding leather shoes, with our hands and faces washed, we would pile into the car, drive the two miles to the otherwise abandoned town centre (well before the era of Sunday shopping) and arrive somewhat harassed and out-of-breath just before, or often just after, the service began.

The service would be traditional and predictable in form: a hymn and a thing, a hymn and a thing, a hymn and a thing. To describe it as conservative would be woefully understated. The first hymn would be rousing: "Let all the world in every corner sing", "To God be the glory, great things he has done..." or "When morning gilds the skies, my heart awaking cries 'May Jesus Christ be praised'". The minister would then lead a prayer and move on to the 'children's talk'. These varied enormously in quality, but would often take the form of a whimsical analogy or extended metaphor, followed by the phrase "And you know, boys and girls, that the Kingdom of God is a little bit like that too...". There was the supermarket shopping analogy, based on the dubious premise that strong-tasting products should not be packed in the same plastic bag in case their flavours rubbed off on each other (did we not have impermeable packaging in the seventies?). I suppose that this was supposed to illustrate, in a round-about way, the dangers of mixing too promiscuously with the unchurched, in case their heathen opinions and habits rubbed off onto you. My favourite children's talk was the fruit and vegetable beauty contest, the candidates in which were the apple, the pear and the potato. Oh how the other fruits and vegetables laughed to see the dull-coloured, mud-flecked potato competing with the lush and shiny red apple and the curvaceous forms of the pear for the title of Fruit and Vegetable Queen! It was not until the judges ordered that they be cut open that the rotten, maggoty cores of the apple and pear were revealed, whereas the potato was flawlessly white and smooth inside and, of course, was declared the winner. "And you know, boys and girls, that the Kingdom of God is a little bit like that too...". The inevitable moral followed, about what you are like inside being more important than how you look on the outside.

The colours black and white were used rather more often than would seem appropriate today to describe spiritual states: one children's talk I remember vividly was about the crucifixion, illustrated by a white cross (Christ's) flanked by two black crosses to illustrate the two criminals crucified on either side. In the next picture, Christ's cross had become black, to illustrate Christ taking the sins of the world onto himself, whereas the penitent thief's had changed from black to white as his sins were forgiven. As the church was located in an almost exclusively white area, there were probably no black people present to take offence, but was it only a generation ago that people with such influence over the minds of the young were playing fast and loose with concepts of white equalling good and black equalling bad?

After the children's talk and another hymn, often one aimed at children, such as "Jesus loves me this I know, for the Bible tells me so" or "Trust and Obey", we would be ushered off to Sunday School in the church hall (euphemistically known for us as "Junior Church", to sweeten the bitter pill of school on a Sunday). Led by a formidable and endlessly enthusiastic woman in her sixties, we sang hymns accompanied on the piano by an elderly lady whom we cruelly nicknamed "Noddy" as what I now assume to be Parkinson's disease started to take its toll on her. We then split up by age into classes, taught by dutiful, often miserable looking Sunday school teachers, all of whom must have had so many better things to do with their time on a Sunday morning. We would read passages from the Bible, recite what were quaintly known as 'memory verses' (Bible verses that it was deemed every child should know by heart, such as John 3:16 "For God so loved the world that He gave His only son, so that whosoever believeth in Him should not perish but have everlasting life"), winning pens or bookmarks adorned with the same verses if we recited correctly. We also had to learn by heart the order of the books of the Bible, and, at one time, I could run through them from Genesis to the Second Book of Kings.

Once a year, a team was chosen from among the Sunday School to represent the church at the town's Bible Quiz. Ten or so teams of children, mostly from the town's Baptist and Methodist churches, would compete for the Bible Quiz crown, being asked questions about a short Bible passage in a game-show style quiz. I was a member of our team two years running, answering questions on the Plagues of Egypt and the Sermon on the Mount, and my father was asked several times to be the question master. Unfortunately, our team never won, but we did enjoy the crisps, cakes and sandwiches laid on for the contestants by the organising church.

How successful was 'Junior Church' in meeting its aims? That depends, of course, on how it defined its own role. As a babysitting service, enabling harassed parents to 'enjoy' the main Sunday morning service in peace, or non-church-going parents to have a few hours' peace at home, it functioned admirably. If, as a Sunday 'school', its intention was to impart knowledge of Christianity, then, again, it certainly worked for me. Thirty years on, I can still find my way around the Bible and discuss Bible stories, characters and doctrines. More controversially and subjectively, was it all about contributing to the raising of well behaved children and moral adults? And, in particular, was its main aim to produce Christian adults? I tend to think that this was indeed its main goal, in which case I suspect that it failed miserably, not only with me but with the vast majority of children who passed through the system at some point in their youth. Does the Church keep records of children attending its youth activities and attempt to link these up with statistics on adult church attendance to measure its success rate? Or does it consider that, as its cause is righteous and unchanging, research of this kind, reminiscent of the customer satisfaction surveys undertaken by companies, would be demeaning, temporal and worldly? I rather suspect the latter, which is unfortunate, as interviews with those, like myself, who were brought up in the church but who have subsequently rejected this way of life would provide useful feedback on what went wrong.

Regular Sunday indoctrination was, of course, complemented by more of the same every morning during assembly at school, with the same messages being promoted, and in many cases the same hymns sung (I later found out that our headmistress was also a Baptist, and at least two of my three teachers at infant school were practising Christians). As my home life reinforced the same values, I assumed as a young child that everyone thought and acted this way.

(Is it right for primary-school-age children to be indoctrinated in any religion at a state school at tax-payers' expense? A six-year-old has no way of knowing that, when the teacher says that five plus five equals ten or that Rome is the capital of Italy, these are undisputed facts, but that when she starts to talk about God or Jesus, this represents a totally different form of education – the transmission of culture rather than fact. There is much to recommend the French system of *laïcité*, whereby church and state are strictly separated, all state institutions – whether schools, hospitals or the civil service – have to remain strictly secular, and state representatives such as teachers and nurses are not supposed to indicate their religion and certainly not to proselytise at work.)

Our family even took several holidays at a Baptist-run hotel, in a seaside resort on the Isle of Wight. While many people, in the 1970s, were busy discovering paella and sangria on the Costas or, the more bourgeois, ciabatta and olives in Tuscany, I considered it entirely normal on holiday to start the morning promptly at nine o'clock with a short time of prayer and Bible study and to round off the day with another short service, followed by an ice-cream-laden strawberry milkshake (for both the adults and the children), which was always greeted as the last word in decadence. These holidays may have been straight-laced, but they were, in fact, also enormous fun for my brother and me, particularly as the leafy hotel grounds were enormous and offered the perfect environment for hide-and-seek, croquet and many other games. We had a particularly successful holiday there in August of 1976, during the famous drought, spending every day playing on the beach and in the rock pools and every evening releasing the crabs we had brought back with us into the hotel lobby.

A contentious issue that never failed to rankle with my brother and me was that, whenever and wherever we were on holiday, we always had to find a local church to attend on Sunday morning. The younger generation of our family (and, I suspect, also my mother) took the view that holidays meant a break from church, too, but my father disagreed and insisted on dragging us to the closest equivalent of a Baptist church wherever in the world we happened to be. Several times whilst on holiday in a predominantly Roman Catholic region of Germany, we schlepped to the local protestant church at my father's insistence, although, as the least linguistically gifted member of the family, he sat through the service not understanding very much at all. Somehow the act of attending church must have given him a satisfaction that transcended the language barrier, but, for the rest of us, the ordeal of church on holiday led to many an argument, with my younger brother in particular digging his heels in and refusing to go, and my father, equally stubbornly, insisting that he had to.

My thoughts and questions at this stage were not the expression of any deep-seated doubts, but rather a way of trying to make sense of the abstract ideas I was being fed. When I look back at my childish questions now, I realise that the doubts I was raising were often more than valid – childish versions of the big philosophical questions which have stumped theologians down the ages:

"So, if God is everywhere, why can't I see him?".

My mother's answer: "Because he's invisible."

"Does that mean that I might bump into him when I'm at church?".

"If you go to Heaven when you die, why does your body get buried first?"

"It's like a box of chocolates – the chocolates are the part of the you that goes to Heaven, and then the box is thrown away."

(Like many supposed answers to religious conundrums, this answer raises more questions than it answers, not least about the viability of floating round bodiless and brainless in Heaven.)

"Why do we have to go to the toilet?"

My father: "What ever do you mean?"

"I mean, couldn't God have designed us better, so we didn't need to?"

(My father thought this question impertinent, but I take the view that it was very reasonable, and I could have added that God should have designed us better to prevent backache, ageing, tooth decay, pain in childbirth, arthritis and many other unpleasant features of life which a benevolent and all-knowing deity should really have foreseen and dealt with in advance.)

My father is an excellent, accomplished public speaker and was often in demand as a Baptist lay-preacher. Every two months or so, he would conduct the service at a small chapel in one of the surrounding villages too small to have its own minister. He would adopt a stern face as he led the (sometimes very small number of) faithful from the pulpit, and it was fascinating, if a little scary, to see my own father in a different role, holding the congregation's attention as his facial expressions and hand gestures told his story. On these occasions, which I very soon started to find onerous, my mother, my brother and I would accompany him, wearing our Sunday best and expected to sit still and behave. We would sit on the hard pews, minding our manners and not fidgeting, listening to a message which, of course, passed a long way above our heads, for what seemed like a very long time.

I started to realise, at around the age of eight or nine, that not everyone's family behaved like mine. My classmates' parents, instead of attending the Graduates' Christian Fellowship or a Bible study group on a Friday evening, went to the pub, or the cinema. They spent Sunday sleeping late or relaxing on the beach in the summer (there was no Sunday shopping at this stage), not rising comparatively early and dressing up in neat shirts and smart trousers to be conveyed to church. In my desire to fit in with my peers, to not be different, I developed a dread of them finding out that I went to Sunday school or, even worse, that my father was a lay preacher! When I complained to my parents that our Sunday church-going risked seriously damaging my credibility at school, they told me, rightly, that any friend who didn't like me any more because I went to church was not worth having in the first place. True enough when it comes to adult friendships, of course, but perhaps not as appropriate for childhood relationships, where fitting in and being one of the crowd are much more important.

My attitude to spiritual matters at this age was mainly one of disinterest. I accepted the compulsory church and Sunday school with resignation – after all, at the age of nine your life is lived in a context of obligatory activities: school from Monday to Friday, accompanying my parents to the supermarket on Saturday afternoons, church on Sunday mornings and often a walk in the woods on Sunday afternoons. As a child, you become used to the lack of power. What would you do with the power if you had it? Once I told my younger brother that God did not exist in order to upset him, in the same way as a child might sadistically tell a younger sibling that Father Christmas is made-up[1]. "But who makes us better when we're sick?" he asked, lower lip quivering. He might well have asked who had arranged the laws of nature in such a way that we fell sick in the first place. I was scolded by my parents for that.

When I remembered, which was not very often, I would say my prayers, tucked up in bed before going to sleep. I was never sure whether to say them aloud or in my head, or indeed whether God could hear them when I did not say them aloud, but, as I shared a bedroom with my brother, the in-the-head version seemed more practical. I was a fearful child, and my prayers consisted mainly of petitions to fend off whatever was frightening me at the time. My parents read the *Daily Mail*, which, then as now, was packed with sensational true-crime stories, and I had an exaggerated idea of how dangerous the world was. Cowering in bed in the dark, shuddering at every noise from outside, I would ask God to protect me from being murdered in my bed by unknown intruders or blown up by an IRA bomb. When, in 1980, the Soviet Union invaded Afghanistan, and, as a consequence, tensions between the superpowers reached boiling point, articles started appearing in the newspapers about the imminent threat of nuclear war. I was terrified, and, convinced that I was unlikely ever to reach adulthood, would for some months regularly beseech God not to let us all perish in a nuclear holocaust.

By the time I reached the age of ten or eleven, my mother had starting working again full-time and there was consequently no time for family prayers at home, and even grace before meals had been shortened to a garbled "Thank you God for breakfast/lunch/tea, Amen". At Sunday school, I answered the questions and learnt my Bible verses dutifully, feeling vaguely that the Sunday morning church obligation was an assault on my free time, but powerless to do anything about it.

Sarah was gorgeous. Seriously so. A year older than me, she had moved from Scotland to our town to live temporarily with her aunt, uncle and cousins, who attended our church. Not only did she have a Scottish accent to die for, she had long, wavy dark hair, huge brown eyes and, although just a year older than me, already at fourteen years old a whiff of adulthood. In absolute terms, she may have been just twelve months older, but her maturity put her far out of my league. She was in my Sunday school class, and, suddenly, church had a new appeal.

13

From the age of 11, I attended single-sex schools, so for a number of years the only place I mixed with girls was at church, and as Nature tends to decree that girls pass through puberty a good year earlier than boys, I found myself, at the age of 13, in a Sunday school class where I was almost the only boy surrounded by a bevy of what seemed to me to be incredibly sophisticated young women.

Sarah, her cousin Lisa, Louise and the other girls in the class were, naturally, one important factor in the transformation of my attitude to religion, but perhaps the most influential people were my two Sunday school teachers at this time, a kindly gentleman of advancing years and a vivacious lady in her mid forties who made Sunday mornings entertaining and stimulating. Having recently moved from primary school to a large and impersonal secondary school where anonymity reigned and, even if the teachers knew who you were, they called you by your surname ("Bennett! Stop chattering and get on with your work!"), it was refreshing to be treated respectfully on a Sunday morning by adults who really did seem interestd in you personally. They cared about our lives, listened to our opinions, let us debate controversial issues (such as the death penalty or why God allowed suffering) and guided our thoughts without laying down an orthodox line. While still not really a pleasure, compulsory church attendance suddenly became much more bearable than it had been.

One Easter, a group of about twenty young teenagers from the church were taken on a three-day sponsored walk around the Kent coast and Canterbury. I went along too, thoroughly enjoying my first ever 'independent' holiday outside the bosom of the family. On the first day we walked along the crest of the White

Cliffs between Folkestone and Dover, enjoying splendid views over the Channel in the spring sunshine, before stopping for the night at Dover youth hostel. The second day's walk was less scenic but still pleasurable, as we tramped along rutted farmyard paths towards our destination, Canterbury youth hostel. By the final day, we all had aching feet and were longing for clean clothes and an arm chair, but overall I had a wonderful time and started to realise that church-going had its advantages, hard pews and boring sermons notwithstanding. The money we raised from the walk was donated to the Baptist Missionary Society and The Evangelical Alliance Relief Fund, and the minister sang our praises from the pulpit, quoting St. Paul's Declaration in the Epistle to the Romans "How beautiful are the feet of them that bring the gospel of peace....".

---

[1] Strangely enough, I can never remember believing in Father Christmas – I don't think our parents encouraged us to do so. Nowadays it seems to be practically compulsory for parents to bang on about Father Christmas, whilst belief in and knowledge of the Christian version of the Christmas story is at an historic low, with surveys suggesting that most children, when asked to name a Christmas Carol, will choose "Rudolph the Red-nosed Reindeer" or "Jingle Bells" rather than "Away in a Manger". It appears that the one supernatural story of Christmas, where Santa, assisted by legions of elves and reindeer, delivers presents to all the world's children on Christmas Eve night, has utterly replaced the other supernatural story involving shepherds, wise men and angels. There are, of course, parallels between the two, particularly the idea that Santa knows how each child has behaved during the year and rewards only the good children (*"He knows when you've been bad or good, so be good for goodness sake…"*).

Conversion

Saint Paul's conversion may have happened from one moment to the next on the Road to Damascus[2], but mine was a gradual process, driven mainly by the desire for everything I wished for to be true, which is perhaps not the best way to make an objective decision. It was December 1983, I was just turning 14, and our church had organised a 'Youth Day' on the Saturday before Christmas. The opportunity to avoid Saturday supermarket shopping with my parents was just too good to miss.

The day was fairly unremarkable: discussions in small groups about the meaning of Christmas, a game in which different teams were given different resources (pens, paper, scissors, paper clips) and asked to 'manufacture' and trade various paper shapes, to illustrate the imbalances in the world economy, and then a short time of prayer and singing to conclude. It was the prayer and singing that caught my imagination. Here were people not much older than me, talking confidently and eloquently to a God in whom they really believed and with whom they felt they had a relationship in some way, in a practical, rather than an abstract, sense. I was used to collective prayers being led from the pulpit by the minister of the church, but this was spiritual democracy in action, with everyone having their own hotline to the Almighty. They prayed using their own words, while sitting cross-legged on the floor, unselfconsciously, without pretence.

Shortly afterwards, I started attending the young people's group that met on Sundays after the evening service. Led by a charismatic young man in his mid twenties, it was experiencing its heyday at around the time I first attended. Fifty or more adolescents and young adults aged between around fourteen and their early twenties would descend on the home of some hapless member of the congregation, often filling the living and dining rooms, perched two or more to an armchair, five or more to a sofa, and spilling out into the hallway and halfway up the stairs. I was one of the youngest there and in awe of these sophisticated youths, much more worldly, but also more other-worldly, than me.

As our unfortunate hosts ran hither and thither making and serving cups of tea and coffee for fifty people, earnest conversations would break out around me (I was generally too shy to participate actively) about science versus religion or the difficulties of being a Christian in a non-Christian home. I now realise how much the content of these conversations was specious or downright immature ("How do we know religion's not true but science is?

They're both just theories, any way!"), but, at the time, they seemed to me the ultimate in profundity.

The meeting proper opened with a prayer and then, to the accompaniment of our leader's guitar, the 'choruses'. As opposed to a hymn, which will normally have several verses, be sung through once from beginning to end and be written for organ or piano accompaniment, a 'chorus' is a short ditty, often just one verse long, designed to be repeated several times. If sung and accompanied properly, it can sometimes induce, after perhaps the third consecutive singing, a trance-like state, a feeling of oneness with God, as if the singer has transcended his or her immediate surroundings to reach some higher plane. Karl Marx was not far wrong when he described religion as "Opium des Volkes" (Opium for the People). For its ability to block out the everyday world and bathe you in a feeling of pure calm, it would be hard to beat a good chorus, accompanied sensitively on the guitar or the piano and sung repeatedly to a slow beat.

Some of these choruses were dreadful and have mercifully been consigned to the scrap-heap, like the faux-archaic and grammatically challenged "It is not I that liveth, but Christ that liveth in me". But some were beautifully crafted little gems. The particularly trance-inducing "Jesus take me as I am", for instance, went:

"Jesus take me as I am.
I can come no other way.
Take me deeper into you.
Make my flesh-life melt away.
Make me like a precious stone,
Crystal clear and finely honed,

Life of Jesus shining through,
Giving glory back to you."
(from "Songs of Fellowship", Kingsway Publications)

The danger, of course, is that, if you can entrance a large group of people just by strumming a few guitar chords and repeating a mantra, they become easy to manipulate. There is no easier way to push through a controversial agenda in a church meeting than to soften up your members in advance with a well-chosen chorus, preferably the superbly manipulative "Bind us together Lord", guaranteed to kill off any opposition or autonomous thought by the end of the first verse. It is the kind of spine-tingling experience generated by any collective singing, experienced by Last-Night-of-the-Prommers belting out "Land of Hope and Glory" or the audience at a Robbie Williams concert singing along to "Angels" whilst waving their cigarette lighters in the air, but, at the time, I was convinced that the aura of tranquillity enveloping me as I closed my eyes and sang was the presence of the Holy Spirit itself.

Yet, however much I was enjoying these new experiences and a new feeling of belonging, I was, even at the age of fourteen, pragmatic enough to realise that the value of the praying, singing and 'fellowship' depended fundamentally on whether or not the underlying belief system was true. Previously, dragged more or less unwillingly to church on a Sunday, the issue of whether or not the whole shebang was true or not had been, at most, of marginal interest, but now I desperately wanted to believe, because I had found a community to which I wanted to belong. With perhaps precocious zeal, I set about, in the footsteps of pilgrims down the ages, establishing the verity of Christianity through my own research.

Twenty years on, and with the benefit of hindsight, I realise that one of the main problems with Christianity is that Jesus, as far as we will ever know, wrote nothing down. Fundamentalists state with absolute conviction that "Jesus said X", whereas in fact all the words attributed to Jesus in the New Testament are highly-edited versions of the recollections of people who may or may not have been eye-witnesses, written down a generation or more after Jesus' death. At best, even if we assume that all those involved had good memories and did not deliberately set out to deceive, the words of Jesus passed through a number of steps before appearing on the page of our present-day Bibles, at each of which the potential for human interference was significant.

1. Jesus talked to his followers, in his native Aramaic. The vast majority of what he said was forgotten and lost for ever, but a tiny proportion was remembered, more or less accurately, by members of Jesus' retinue. It is likely that even this tiny proportion was altered slightly to make memorising it easier.

2. A generation later, many eye-witnesses accounts were circulating, with sayings attributed to Jesus, presumably in the original Aramaic. Some of them came to the attention to the Gospel writers. At this stage, the actual words attributed to Jesus had probably changed, even if their sense had been retained (can you recall, word-for-word, what someone said to you just last week, let alone twenty years ago?). The Gospel writers edited this mass of information, cherry-picked the elements that fitted in

with their narrative, ignored the parts that they did not understand or which did not fit in with what they wanted to say, and translated the text into Greek.

3. Throughout the first few centuries AD, the corpus of texts about Jesus was edited, with certain Gospels (for instance the Gospel of Thomas) meeting with disfavour and being declared heretical, and others (the Gospels of Matthew, Mark, Luke and John) being given the seal of orthodoxy. Given the lack of recording equipment and documentation at that time, decisions on which versions of Jesus' history were valid must have been taken mainly on political, rather than historical grounds.

4. The Greek New Testament is translated into modern languages. For most readers of this book, this means English.

So, by the time the text appears on the page before you, it has undergone extensive editing and at least two translations. Instead of saying "Jesus said 'I am the way, the truth an the life'" it would be more accurate to say that He said something which was translated and was then translated again to finally be rendered as 'I am the way, the truth and the life' in English, a realisation that cannot help but cast doubt on exactly what He meant when He said it.

(It appears to be mainly Christians who insist on quoting their holy book in a translation of a translation. Moslems spend years studying classical Arabic so that they can read the Quran in the original – translations into modern languages are considered to be little more than glossaries or sources of reference and are often accompanied by the Arabic text in a bilingual version. I recently attended a thirteen-year-old Jewish boy's Bar Mitzvah in Canada and was intrigued to discover that, despite his tender years, he had already been studying Hebrew with a private tutor for five years and was able to read aloud from the Torah and lead some of the prayers in Hebrew – unlike many Christians in the English-speaking world, who quote their English Bible as authoritative (most famously Miriam Amanda "Ma" Ferguson, the first female governor of Texas, who is alleged to have stated that "if the King's English was good enough for Jesus, it's good enough for me!").

Given that the life of Christ takes on cosmic significance for Christians and is considered by them to be the most important event in human history, you would have thought that it could have been better planned. If Jesus had only written His own thoughts down, we would know that they were really His, in the same way that we know St Paul's ideas are really his own. And, given the antiquity of the Earth and the length of time that passed before His coming, you would have thought that the Redeemer's entry into human history could have been delayed for just a couple of thousand years so that "The Greatest Story Ever Told" could have been properly documented, filmed and audio-recorded to leave future generations in no doubt about its authenticity. Instead we are left with a highly-edited collection of attributions and third-party opinions which provide a fascinating insight into Jewish first century thought but cannot sensibly be taken as constituting ultimate truth, the definitive stage in the development of human spiritual and ethical philosophy, as evangelicals[3] would have us believe.

At the time, I was very much influenced by C.S. Lewis's famous 'trilemma', the so-called "Mad, Bad or God" argument, which goes like this.

'I am trying here to prevent anyone saying the really foolish thing that people often say about Him: 'I'm ready to accept Jesus as a great moral teacher, but I don't accept His claim to be God.' That is one thing we must not say. A man who was merely a man and said the sort of thing Jesus said would not be a great moral teacher. He would either be a lunatic — on a level with the man who says he is a poached egg — or else he would be the Devil of Hell. You must make your choice. Either this man was, and is, the Son of God: or else a madman or something worse. You can shut Him up for a fool, you can spit at Him and kill him as a demon or you can fall at his feet and call Him Lord and God. But let us not come with any patronizing nonsense about His being a great human teacher. He has not left that open to us. He did not intend to.' *C.S. Lewis*, from *Mere Christianity*.

In retrospect, with twenty years' more life experience under my belt, I realise that the objections to this line of argument are twofold. As shown above, there is no handy "Gospel according to Jesus" in which Christ makes claims about himself – all we know about Him passed from eye witnesses into folklore and was subsequently written down in edited form and translated, leaving ample room for hyperbole and over-interpretation to creep in and words He did not say to be placed in His mouth, as happened to the hapless 'Brian' in the Monty Python film. Secondly, it is quite possible to be deluded in your religious and spiritual beliefs, as almost all people living in pre-scientific societies are, and still have something valuable to say. In fact, it would be only a slight exaggeration to state that, before the late Renaissance, the era of Galileo, absolutely everyone was totally ignorant and spectacularly wrong in their beliefs about how the universe was structured, and that, before Darwin, almost everyone was wildly deluded about the evolution of life. It would appear, from reading the *Canterbury Tales*, that Geoffrey Chaucer believed in astrology, that the mutual alignment of the stars and planets had a bearing on the outcome of human lives on Earth, but this does not detract from Chaucer's greatness. We accept that people living in the Middle Ages had medieval beliefs. The current Dalai Lama holds what many would consider to be absurd beliefs as far as reincarnation is concerned, for example, and has officially recognised a six-year-old Tibetan boy as the reincarnation of the tenth Panchen Lama, but his teachings on peace, happiness and spiritual fulfilment speak to millions, and no one could justifiably accuse him of having evil intent or being 'on a level with the man who says he is a poached egg'.

Such pragmatic doubts did not deter me aged fourteen as I ploughed my way through the relevant tomes in the school library. I wanted to believe, indeed I felt that my future happiness depended on it, so I did not approach my quest for truth from the most objective of angles. I felt that the questions which needed to be answered were: *What did Jesus believe about himself and why would He lie?* And *Did He really come back to life after the crucifixion?* I took as my starting point that people do not usually lie unless there is some (pecuniary or other) advantage in so doing. So why would Jesus lie about himself? As far as I could see, his words brought him little in the way of benefits – indeed they led ultimately to His execution on the Cross. And why would His disciples lie about having seen Him after the Resurrection or about the other 'miracles' they allegedly witnessed? Following Jesus after His death brought them into collision with the Roman authorities, so they must have believed that their story was true. And, if Jesus did indeed die and His body was taking by the Roman authorities, why did they not simply present it as soon as rumours of the resurrection started to circulate? Wilfully ignoring the obvious difficulty that almost all of my evidence came from the same source (i.e. the Gospels) and lacked external corroboration, I decided that the most likely explanation for the sequence of events was that Jesus was indeed divine, did rise from the dead and that therefore Christianity was true. Quite a few leaps in logic, but for someone who wishes to believe, none of them individually insurmountable.

(Is it not amazing how the brain is so keen to accept information that supports a preconceived position and to filter out any information that would challenge it? Psychologist Cordelia Fine, writing in the Guardian on 26 January 2006, pointed out that "evidence that fits with our beliefs is quickly waved through the mental border control, while counter-evidence must submit to close interrogation and, even then, will probably not be admitted. As a result, people can end up holding their beliefs even more strongly after seeing counter-evidence." What an accurate description of my conversion.)

The next question was what to do with my new-found belief system. Evangelical Christianity is different from many other religions in that it sets little store by the fact of having been born into it. It is not bound up with your nationhood or your ethnic identity in the same way as, say, Roman Catholicism or Greek

Orthodoxy. Almost all Greeks are Orthodox, it defines them as a nation and is an important part of each person's 'Greekness'. If you are Greek, whether or not you believe the Greek Orthodox take on God and the after-life is of only marginal importance, and even Greeks who are agnostic in their religious views and have not actively practised for years would never consider 'opting out' or changing their religion. It is simply not an option, as to do so would also be a renunciation of their roots. Greeks do not 'convert' to Orthodoxy, they are simply born Greek and follow the Church's rites from their baptism through to their funeral. But being born into an evangelical Christian family is not considered enough to be a Christian. Emphasis is placed on the importance of personal conversion, of "making a decision for Christ" or "inviting Jesus into your heart". Our minister would regularly remind us that "God only has children, no grandchildren", meaning that merely coming from a Christian background was no substitute for a personal conversion experience of the kind described vividly by Charles Wesley in his masterfully crafted hymn "And can it be…":

"Long my imprisoned spirit lay, fast bound in sin and nature's night;

Thine eye diffused a quickening ray;

I woke, the dungeon flamed with light;

My chains fell off, my heart was free,

I rose, went forth, and followed thee. "

I could almost picture some kind of spiritual Jesus entering my "soul", located in some undisclosed part of my brain, and from there directing my behaviour. One very emotional Sunday evening, after returning from the youth meeting, I tearfully prayed to God to "come into my life" and believed He had done so. I awoke the following morning convinced I was "a new creation".

As I attended a Baptist church, the logical next step was to be baptised. Unlike Anglican or Catholic churches, which usually baptise babies and young children, the Baptist church practises "adult" baptism, which, in practice, means that those wishing to undergo the ritual must be old enough to request it themselves, allegedly in full knowledge of what it means and entails. My brother and I had both been "dedicated" at the church when just a few months old, but this informal ceremony was more for our parents to promise before God to bring us up properly in a Christian environment than to convey any supernatural blessing or protection on the child.

Baptismal services were the highlights of our church's calendar, the only time when our normally sober minister would ratchet up the emotional content of the service to the level of a Billy Graham rally or a Deep South revivalist meeting and, as the organist banged out the chords to "I am trusting thee, Lord Jesus", members of the congregation touched by the spectacle would make their tearful way to the front pew, the first stage in their own baptismal journey.

"Candidates", as they were known, were baptised in the baptismal pool at the front of the church where, in an Anglican church, the altar would have stood. Normally a raised, carpeted platform, on baptismal Sundays the carpet would be rolled back and a trapdoor opened to reveal a small pool some three metres long by two metres wide and deep enough for an adult to stand in waist-deep water. The minister would leave the church during the singing of the hymn before the baptism, returning dressed, somewhat comically, in a knee-length white gown over waist-high fisherman's rubber boots. Having waded out to the centre of the pool, he would invite the candidates one after another to stand before him. "Do you accept the Lord Jesus Christ as your own personal Saviour and Lord?" he would ask, to which the orthodox response was "I do." With the words "I therefore baptise you in the name of the Father, the Son and the Holy Spirit. Amen" he would then tip candidates backwards into the water until they were totally immersed and then pull them back to a standing position. The symbolism could not be clearer. Like Christ, who died, was buried and then raised, so the candidate's old life was 'buried' under the water and he rose again to a new existence.

I was baptised on 25 November 1984, a few weeks before my fifteenth birthday [completely coincidentally, my first child was born, to the day, twenty years later]. I remember it as an emotional and intensely experienced rite of passage, followed by several days of anti-climax.

---

[2] "Now as he journeyed he approached Damascus, and suddenly a light from Heaven flashed about him", Acts of the Apostles 9:3 (RSV)

[3] According to the Collins English Dictionary, an evangelical is a member of a protestant church which "emphasises the importance of personal conversion and faith in atonement through the death of Christ as a means of salvation." It is often used to denote the more conservative elements of a particular denomination, in particular those who interpret the Bible literally, and that is how I have used the word in this book.

Fervour

My fervent years had begun. When I look back on how I used to think during that time, it strikes me how adolescent evangelical Christianity is. Both teenagers and evangelical Christians share the same certainty that they are right, that they have discovered something which wiser and more experienced people have managed to overlook. Both groups love to polarise the world into extremes of right or wrong, black or white, and have little time for the complexities which characterise our lives as adult human beings. They are also idealistic, confusing the ideal way with the only way, the perfect outcome with the only possible outcome, and are reluctant to make compromises or settle for the best practical result. One of the ways that adolescents become adults is by starting to realise that the black-and-white world view they have constructed is, in fact, a gross over-simplification, and that reality is much more complex than it first appears. They start to see the other sides of arguments, to be less judgemental, to develop nuanced views. They realise that life is about compromises, that perfection is not always possible. Unfortunately, evangelical Christianity offers no similar mechanism – at the age of twenty five or thirty five you are still expected to accept the same Manichean picture as you did when you were fifteen, and to categorise the world in simplistic black and white couplets: Christian/ Unchristian, Sin/ Virtue, Saved/Unsaved, Heaven/Hell, Angels/Demons, God/Satan. For every abstract, supernatural concept, there is an equal and opposite concept, but no gradation or middle ground in between – the condition described by Richard Dawkins as "the tyranny of the discontinuous mind".

To be fair, the church I attended until the age of seventeen was broad enough to accept differing points of view, and some of the youth leaders with whom I had the most contact were intelligent people not afraid of presenting a difficult subject (such as the six-day creation versus gradual evolution over geological time, or the existence of suffering) and inviting us to consider the various possible interpretations. Discussion was encouraged, and different points of view valued, "teaching" was eschewed in favour of exploration and nurture. Perhaps most importantly, no one was ever put down for stating an unorthodox point of view.

I continued to attend the youth meetings, where we sang the same choruses, but somehow the ecstatic experience brought on by the worship was never of the same intensity as it had been in the beginning. It remained, annoyingly, just slightly out of my reach.

Like many other things in life, the novelty gradually wore off, to be replaced by a feeling of ordinariness, the realisation that this was what I did every Sunday. It became a form of addiction, essential to strengthen me to cope with the following week, especially as I was unhappy at school at this time and my O-level examinations were fast approaching.

Every so often, the topic of the Sunday evening youth meeting would be sex, and, more precisely, why you shouldn't be doing it. Many people assume that abstinence movements such as the American "Silver Ring Thing" are twenty-first century phenomena, but twenty years or so ago, in the mid 1980s, very similar messages were being promoted to Christian teenagers here in the UK. These talks always started with an affirmation that sex was good, that God approved of it and had indeed created it himself, although it was quickly emphasised that only affection-based sex with a partner of the opposite gender in the context of a faithful, lifelong marriage was "good", preferably for the purpose of procreation. In keeping with the evangelical tradition that tries to divide the world neatly into black and white opposites, God was assumed to hate and condemn any other sexual behaviour which did not fit into this narrow definition: pre-marital and extra-marital sex, casual sex, serial monogamy, gay and lesbian sex, divorce and remarriage and in fact any behaviour apart from faithful, lifelong marriage, which He just about tolerated. However, it would appear that He even found this way of life too messy for His own Son, who is assumed to have been a lifelong celibate (although the gap in the biblical records of His life, between the ages of 13, when He visits the Temple in Jerusalem, and 30, when He starts His ministry, fills me with suspicion), and Jesus' mother Mary, who apparently became pregnant by the Holy Spirit whilst still a virgin and, if you are Roman Catholic, was herself conceived supernaturally. This teaching led at least one teenage couple in the youth group to marry at an extremely early age (she was just seventeen), with disastrous results when they separated soon afterwards, splitting up another engaged couple in their wake.

At other meetings, the emphasis was on "witnessing", jargon for telling your friends about your faith. Indeed, one Easter we all went away for a youth weekend at a boarding school in East Sussex to be indoctrinated for 48 hours in the secrets of "witnessing". "Why witness?" was the title of the opening session, and the answer given was "Because your faith is like a cheque – it is worth nothing until you give it away…". Never was an emptier analogy used, but we swallowed it unquestioningly. It was taken as self-evident that, rather than being Sunday-only Christians, we should act as living advertisements for Christianity throughout the week, in our conduct, but also in our discussions with our friends (and family, if not already churchgoers). I dutifully witnessed whenever I could, even wearing a stylised ixthos fish on my school blazer lapel to encourage my classmates to ask leading questions about my faith. I thought then that I argued persuasively, but I never managed to convince any of my friends even to accompany me to church youth club, let alone to "bring them to Christ" (I should count my blessings that at least none of the youth leaders at that church was crass enough to suggest that we should witness to our friends to save them from perdition – in the next church I attended (see the following chapter) that would have been the first reason given).

At school, I joined the Christian Union, which initially met once a week at Friday lunchtime but was soon organising daily prayer meetings at morning break in a curious cupboard-sized room which shared a glass wall with the prefects' common room. Theoretically, it was led by the chemistry master, a shy man who was more than content to let the members run their own show, which meant, inevitably, that those with the most forceful personalities took over. A leader soon emerged – a pious, arrogant boy with a condescending manner and unflinching belief in his own inerrancy, the product of the most fundamentalist church in town. Many more moderate members fled when he suggested that we should be speaking in tongues, taking communion and conducting healings in Christian Union meetings which, thanks to the glass wall of the room in which they were held, soon became semi-public demonstrations of piety. His second-in-command was a quiet, contemplative boy who seemed permanently to be struggling with his internal demons, whatever they might have been. He appeared to be always on the verge of tears, and his version of Christianity was a joyless one, with much self-abasement and self-loathing. He went to the same fundamentalist church, where belief in miracles was commonplace, and one day arrived at school not wearing his chunky spectacles, declaring that his myopia had been "healed" at Sunday service. "Congratulations!" I exclaimed, shaking him by the hand but unsure whether congratulation was the correct etiquette for someone who had just been supernaturally healed. I asked tentatively whether this meant that he could now see perfectly. "Oh no," he replied. "I've been healed but it hasn't taken effect yet…". After a week of screwing up his eyes to try and read what was written on the blackboard, he sheepishly started wearing an old pair of spectacles again, no doubt castigating himself inside for not having had enough faith to transform his "healing" into reality. I felt very sad for him.

It would be no exaggeration to say that, in those days, I was obsessed. Christianity filled my thoughts during the day and my dreams at night. At a time when I should perhaps have been developing my social life, listening to loud music, rebelling against my elders and thinking about my forthcoming adulthood, I spent my time mulling over aspects of doctrine I did not fully understand, difficulties and contradictions I had found when reading my Bible (not a sensible thing to do unsupervised) or doubts festering at the back of my mind. I spent more time than was healthy reading 'inspirational' books, generally featuring heroes who had overcome great odds with the aid of their faith, such as Brother Andrew, a missionary in the Far East, who smuggled Bibles into China, New York gang member Nicky Cruz or Corrie ten Boom, a Dutch woman from Haarlem who sheltered Jews in her home during the Second World War[4], or listening to 'Christian' music. Rather like a drug addict always in search of the next high, I continued to chase the euphoria, the feeling of oneness with God, which I had experienced initially, as a new Christian, but it remained, annoyingly, just out of reach.

For a while, I kept a 'prayer diary', a notebook with each page divided into two columns. On the left I would record my prayers on a particular subject and, on the right, the answer to those prayers. Amazingly, most of my petitions to God seemed to be answered fairly quickly, but then I only ever asked for things which were likely to happen in the normal run of events. An entry on the left might read "Prayed that I would find my PE kit" and the corresponding answer on the right would state "Found in the cupboard under the stairs!". It's a miracle! In retrospect, I should have divided the page into four columns: one for my prayers, one for prayers answered, one for prayers remaining unanswered and the last one for situations which sorted themselves anyway without having to be prayed about in advance.

God's intervention in the world through answered prayer is an article of faith for evangelical Christians, most of whom seem to have little idea about how to estimate the probability of something happening. Happy to attribute every improvement in their circumstances to God's miraculous intervention, they fail to take into account all those times when God did not intervene or when their circumstances, following normal fluctuations and rhythms, improved anyway. They find it difficult to understand that, in a large enough population, over a long enough period, the most extraordinary coincidences are likely to occur, resulting merely from the law of probabilities.

Take, for example, the so-called Diana Prophecy. In May of 1997, a 43-year-old woman from Sheffield claimed to have had a 'Word from the Lord' in which she saw people laying flowers on the streets. She told the minister of her church, but thought little more about it until Diana, Princess of Wales died on 31 August of the same year, and a nation in mourning expressed its sorrow by laying flowers in front of the royal palaces in London. The belief that Diana's death had been prophesied and was somehow a sign from the Lord led to a short-lived charismatic revival later that year.

However, a back-of-an-envelope calculation gives the lie to this extraordinary claim. How many charismatic churches are there in the UK? If each middle-sized town has at least one, then there must be around a thousand. How often do the members of these churches claim to receive 'Words from the Lord'. My own experience of this type of church is that at least one 'Word from the Lord' will be received at each Sunday service. So a thousand or more visions are being claimed every week, up and down the UK, or many tens of thousands every year. In that case, would it not be extraordinary if at least one or two of them did not appear to predict real events, just by the law of probabilities?

By the age of sixteen, I had been a Christian for around two years. By this stage, I was beginning to suspect that some aspects of the faith I had espoused were rather less savoury than I had initially thought. My first real disappointment was the "Great White Throne" debacle.

The "Great White Throne" was the theme of the sermon preached by an American evangelist, at that time running a church in the Netherlands, who visited our town for a weekend mission one summer at the invitation of the church choir master. The young people's group was abuzz – this was one of the most exciting events to have happened in a long time. For weeks in advance, we practised songs and musical numbers, rehearsed sketches and learnt poems for the event, to which we were encouraged to invite all our friends, especially those who attended the church youth club on Friday evenings, felt by some church members to be suspiciously secular.

The great day arrived, we all ate supper together in the church hall, prayed earnestly for 'seeds to be sown' in the hearts and minds of our visitors, and then let the proceedings commence. We sang our choruses, the band played, we performed our sketches, our audience clapped along and laughed in all the right places, and we thought the evening would turn out to be a success. Then the evangelist took his place in the pulpit and began to speak.

The sermon wasn't just long – 'long' does not begin to do it justice. It felt interminable, even to those like me had been accustomed to sitting through religious services since their earliest childhood. Slowly, the friends who had been invited to the event started to trickle away, until a tipping point was reached and they all, without exception, bolted for the doors. I thought the preacher would change tack as he started to lose his audience, but he ploughed on manfully with the sermon he had set out to preach, labouring each point, as his audience voted with its feet, leaving only the regular churchgoers still in the pews. At this point, the atmosphere was ratcheted up a notch, as the sermon reached its climax, the "Great White Throne of Judgement"[5] before which all would stand on Doomsday. The non-Christians were fortunate enough to have left by this point, but, together with the other regular attenders still present, I was treated to my first hellfire and brimstone sermon. Before that day, my God had been a kind, loving, forgiving, paternal figure — most importantly, in the turmoil of my early adolescence, *someone who made me feel safe*. I had responded freely to what I thought was an unconditional gospel of love, freely offered by a generous God. The idea that anyone should be bullied or threatened into a relationship with Christ or should enter into that relationship from a position of fear was an anathema to me. That day, I learnt for the first time about the darker, threatening, more sadistic side of Christianity, and was confronted with the unpalatable fact that today's Christianity, even when wrapped up in modernity, is the child of the medieval church, the behemoth that ruled Europe by fear from the first century after Christ until the Renaissance and beyond. It was the first time that my innocent, childish faith had been abused.

---

[4] At the time, I naively lapped up these thrilling tales, packed with derring-do, miraculous healings and conversions, failing to notice that they had all been ghost-written by the same husband-and-wife team, John and Elizabeth Sherrill, referred to without a hint of hyperbole as "God's chosen writers" at http://across.co.nz/GodsChosenWriters.htm. So that's why the miracles described in all three books seemed so alike! Incidentally, these simplistic texts, staple fare for evangelical Christians, are often accorded levels of reverence normally reserved for Holy Writ.

[5] *Revelation 20:11 Then I saw a great white throne and him who was seated on it. Earth and sky fled from his presence, and there was no place for them. 12 And I saw the dead, great and small, standing before the throne, and books were opened. Another book was opened, which is the book of life. The dead were judged according to what they had done as recorded in the books. 13 The sea gave up the dead that were in it, and death and Hades gave up the dead that were in them, and each person was judged according to what he had done. 14 Then death and Hades were thrown into the lake of fire. The lake of fire is the second death. 15 If anyone's name was not found written in the book of life, he was thrown into the lake of fire.*

Rock and Religion

I was seventeen when my family decided to move church, after attending the town's main Baptist church for fifteen years. My brother, then aged thirteen, was already putting up spirited resistance against the once-weekly ordeal of sitting through a ninety-minute service every Sunday evening, especially as the minister at that time lacked spontaneity, and Sunday services had become a series of items on an order-of-service sheet. So we decided to attend our local Baptist chapel, located in our part of town, just a mile away from our home. We had the impression that this church would offer an altogether more lively Sunday-morning experience, and we were not disappointed. Guitars were strummed, hands clapped, hips swayed and arms stretched heavenwards as chorus followed chorus. This was more like it. My brother and I were hooked. Church was suddenly fun and spontaneous. We were, of course, too naïve to realise that the golden, and counter-intuitive, rule applied here too: the more freedom a church encourages in its worship, the more narrow will be its doctrines and the more free thought will be considered subversive.

Without realising it, beguiled by all the rock music, dancing and clapping, we were about to exchange our rather staid but fairly enlightened church for a much more narrow-minded, fundamentalist environment, where the harshest doctrines were forced on those least able to resist.

We duly changed churches and, within a few months, became full members of the Baptist chapel. Initially we enjoyed the change. As it was located just along the road, the chapel was attended by people living in our immediate neighbourhood, which increased the social possibilities for my brother and me. It was also much smaller, which meant that we went from being small fish in a fairly big pond to being the new boys in a more intimate social group. We immediately made friends, including girlfriends within a few months. On Sunday mornings we looked forward to heading up the road to meet our pals and joining in the singing and clapping.

My brother soon joined the "Sunday club", yet another euphemism for Sunday school, held during the second part of the morning service. It was a welcome escape from having to sit through the weekly sermon so, even though at seventeen I was rather too old for it, I started attending too. The class was taken by a kindly gentleman in his fifties, who seldom had a word to say, and Sheila, a highly-strung woman in her forties, one of the most intensely religious people I have ever known. Her eyes burned with all the fervour of those who have no doubt, convinced of the truth of their message. Her message to the teenagers in her care was stark, harsh and left no room for subtleties: the Bible was God's word, every last dot and comma of it (including the English translation, presumably), to be interpreted literally in all cases. Everyone was destined for the fiery furnace unless Jesus saved them, and He would only do that if you "gave your life to him" (so not much room for manoeuvre there). Britain was no longer a Christian country because homosexuality between consenting adults had been made legal in the late 1960s. Young people should sit quietly in church and learn from their elders. Sheila was seldom to be seen reading a copy of The Guardian – the term "bleeding-heart liberal" would not often be used to describe her.

Perhaps the most outrageous assertion with which she regaled us concerned a passage in the Old Testament where God curses a sinner for some misdemeanour and warns that the curse will apply not only to the object of His wrath but also to all his descendants. "And, even today, that man's descendants are living under God's curse," said Sheila, neglecting to mention how her rigorous moral code could possibly allow her to worship a vengeful deity who was still punishing people for the sins that their ancestors had supposedly committed almost three thousand years previously. Imagine some poor member of Jewish diaspora today suffering misfortune after misfortune as God continues to punish him for the sins of his distant ancestor – such an idea is as preposterous as it is cruel, yet this was the way Sheila taught her charges to interpret the Bible.

She was, undoubtedly, convinced of the righteousness of her cause, but how can filling the minds of young teenagers (most of those in the class were only 13 or 14) with Hell and damnation possibly be justified? Surely puberty and early adolescence are difficult enough to cope with here on Earth, with the physical changes happening to your body and the chemical changes in your brain, without being force-fed violent images of pain and torture in an abstract world to come. As far as I know, none of the members of that class still attends a church – perhaps they are still too angry about having a difficult time of their life made even more distressing by the poisonous doctrine being fed to us in Sunday School.

A year or so later, she decided to give up teaching the class but, true to form, convinced herself that God had told her "that it is time to move on". Her almost tearful announcement was greeted by derision by my younger brother, who even then was much more healthily sceptical than me. "Why couldn't she just say that she couldn't be arsed to teach us every Sunday morning? Why did she have to make out that God *told* her to do it?" he complained. He thought she was being insincere, but I believe that she honestly thought she had a hotline to the Almighty and that He told her what to do on an ongoing basis.

Free thinking was not encouraged. Sheila once told us, when my brother objected to one of her outrageous statements, that "This is a Sunday school class, and you're hear to learn. It's not a debating society." The doctrines we were force-fed were of the narrowest and strictest kind. Another youth leader told us that "We don't know exactly how ancient the Earth is, but it's around 4000 years old", without a hint that this figure may have been just a tiny bit controversial. You were either a Christian or you weren't – there was no grey area in between. Indeed, nuances, grey areas or any uncertainties were frowned upon as being the luxury of those who lacked faith. Certain things were true, however outrageous they seemed, and if you didn't believe them, you had jolly well better get down on your knees and start praying for more faith to do so. Like the Queen of Hearts in Alice in Wonderland, we were encouraged to believe "six impossible things before breakfast" as a sign of our faith.

The minister of our church was a sensible man, moderate in his views, and his sermons provoked little controversy, but, on the eight or so Sundays a year when he was on holiday and invited another minister or lay person to take his place in the pulpit, we endured a selection of crackpots and oddities, each of whom was more reactionary than the one before. One lay preacher, taking the service at the time of the 400th anniversary of the Spanish Armada in 1988, told the congregation that God had been on England's side whenever the country had been at war, and no more so than in 1588 when the evil tide of Spanish Catholicism had been turned back at England's shores. (If he gave that sermon today, he would no doubt fall foul of New Labour's new "incitement to religious hatred" legislation.)

We had to endure the elderly preacher whose sermon was on the famous story of Balaam's talking ass[6], who left us in no doubt that we were meant to believe that this human-asinine conversation literally had taken place, and the one who described his missionary activities amongst the godless (read 'Roman Catholic') Austrians as though he had been working with a tribe of head-shrinkers in darkest Peru.

Another elderly lay-preacher was accompanied by his wife, an overly made-up, manicured and big-haired American singer with high-powered shoulder pads called Mary-Lou who almost bounced off the walls of the chapel with enthusiasm (imagine a devotional version of Dolly Parton on speed) as she led the congregation in singing a selection of her songs, including the patriotic "Come, Britain, back to God!" and a song supposedly for children entitled "I only want to know about Jesus the Son of God", which contained the disturbing couplet "We don't want to go to Hell when we die/We're going up with Jesus and living in the sky…". Fortunately, they just don't write them like that any more. My father, not usually one to fritter away his money on music, was persuaded to shell out five pounds ninety nine for a cassette of Mary-Lou's greatest hits and, for some time afterwards, would briskly perform his morning exercises to the frenetic strains of "I will be *HAPPY* in the God of my salvation! I will be *HAPPY* in the Lord!", a song which my brother would also delight in playing for the amusement of his friends.

On occasions, my brother and I could not resist the temptation to mercilessly lampoon our fellow worshippers and we would set about writing a short play or an alternative notice sheet satirising them. One Harvest Festival, when the church was collecting money to send a lorry-load of provisions to a poor community in Romania, we wrote, photocopied and sold in support a play entitled "*The Vladibostovic Saga*" in which various thinly disguised characters from the chapel were sent on a top-secret mission to save a church located in the midst of the Siberian wastes from a dangerous cult known as the "Wavy-Handies". Few of the church hierarchy escaped our pens and, despite the fact that the play was liberally sprinkled with low-level sexual innuendo, the minister was broadminded enough to give it his cautious backing, and we sold enough copies to raise a modest amount of money for the mission.

---

[6] Then the LORD opened the mouth of the donkey, and it said to Balaam, "What have I done to you, that you have struck me these three times?" Balaam said to the donkey, "Because you have made a fool of me! I wish I had a sword in my hand! I would kill you right now!" But the donkey said to Balaam, "Am I not your donkey, which you have ridden all your life to this day? Have I been in the habit of treating you this way?" And he said, "No." Then the LORD opened the eyes of Balaam, and he saw the angel of the LORD standing in the road, with his drawn sword in his hand; and he [Balaam] bowed down, falling on his face. (Numbers 22:28-31)

Zealotry and doubt

In the aftermath of the London terrorist bombings of July 2005, it was reported that, over the previous decade, British universities had become hotbeds of Islamic radicalism and a training ground for potential Islamist terrorists. This did not surprise me. At university, particularly if you live on campus, rather than outside in the 'real world', it is possible to surround yourself with likeminded fellow students for almost every waking hour. In such circumstances, it is all too easy for faith groups in particular to turn in on themselves and develop their own versions of orthodoxy legitimated by continuous reciprocal confirmation within the group. When I started university in 1988, I soon discovered that, should I wish to, I could attend at least a couple of Christian meetings every day and spend the rest of my time (apart from lectures) relaxing in the comfortable, well-equipped chaplaincy.

And some people did just that. With a wide range of groups to choose from to suit every theological taste, from the liberal Student Christian Movement (known by its abbreviation SCM – other, more evangelical, Christian students quipped cattily that it stood for "Slightly Christian Marxists"), through the intriguingly named GITS (Growing in the Spirit) group to the Christian Union, which became significantly more rightwing and fundamentalist as my student days progressed, you could easily fill most of your spare time with Bible study groups, prayer meetings, third-world lunches (where you ate just bread and cheese and gave the amount you would otherwise have spent on your meal to charity) and other devotional activities, avoiding the need to mix with the 'unsaved' except at lectures.

My social life was more varied than that, but I still attended at least five Christian meetings a week, the largest of which was the main Christian Union meeting on a Tuesday evening. Several hundred students crammed into the chaplaincy to sing choruses, pray and listen to the 'teaching', which actually meant being berated by a different social conservative each week telling us why we shouldn't have sex before marriage ("No sex please, we're Christians?" was the total of one meeting, the question mark suggesting, wrongly, that there might be some debate on the subject) or why we needed to keep ourselves apart ('holy') from the permissive society that surrounded us. By my last year of university, the Christian Union had taken to meeting in a hall in the university's affiliated teaching-training college, allegedly so that the (mostly female) trainee teachers no longer had to walk along a dimly lit path to the main campus, but unofficially because some members felt that the chaplaincy, with its non-denominational atmosphere (even the Jewish Society met there!)

had become too heathen a venue. It had also withdrawn from the Students' Union and was no longer allowed to use its premises. Depending on whom you asked, the falling-out had been due either to the CU not wishing its membership subscriptions to contribute to funding information on abortion, or to the Students' Union considering the CU's constitution to be discriminatory, as those wishing to join had to sign a statement of faith in Christ and adherence to biblical principles.

Christian Union members also met on another evening of the week in "cell groups". The name had nothing to do with prisons but, intriguingly, with the communist idea of creating cells at grass-roots level throughout society to prepare for a future revolution. In these groups of eight or so people, squeezed into someone's student room, we studied the Bible, prayed and drank copious amounts of tea. In my final year, I also lusted, in vain, after Holly, the cell group member in whose room we met. The atmosphere in these groups was unvaryingly right-wing, socially conservative and fundamentalist, despite their apparently informality, and, as they offered the opportunity to get to know the other members in more depth than would be possible during Christian Union meetings, I often found out more than I wished to about the unsavoury views of my fellow 'cell mates'.

On Wednesday afternoons, we went to the Anglican chaplain's home for the Growing in the Spirit or 'GITS' group, a refreshingly open, undogmatic meeting focusing on the individual's search for God rather than on 'teaching' from the Bible. The chaplain was an extraordinary woman, full of life and warmth, open and broadminded, and increasingly frustrated by the limitations imposed upon her as a woman by the Anglican hierarchy, particularly as, at that time, women were still not allowed to be ordained. She once shared with us her anger at being allowed to take the entire Sunday morning service, including Communion, but having had to find an ordained man to bless the Eucharist bread and wine in advance. I assume that she has since been ordained and become a successful parish priest.

It was this chaplain who organised visits to a young offenders' institution located close to the university. On my first visit, I was suitably awestruck by the height and width of the perimeter walls, the body searches, the doors closing and locking behind you leaving you trapped in a small lobby area before the door in front was buzzed open to let you through. We would help the prison chaplain to take the evening service, attended by a surprisingly shy and polite group of inmates. The institution's turnover was rapid, as most of the young men had received relatively short sentences, and the prison chaplain's strategy was to interest them in Christianity so as to be able to link them with a local church upon their release. Our role, as students of around the same age, was to demonstrate that church was not attended exclusively by elderly ladies in hats. I'm sure I learned and gained more from the experience that any of the young inmates ever did.

With Catholic Society on Sunday evenings (which was more about sitting around chatting and eating pasta than anything particularly Catholic), the service in the chaplaincy on Sunday morning and occasional prayer meetings during the week, it was easy to live exclusively in a Christian bubble that would be difficult to recreate in any environment other than a university, or possibly a monastery or convent. These closed environments, where, should you wish, you can talk to the same people about the same subjects interminably, and the outside world is easily excluded, can provide ideal conditions for the development of religious fervour and, in some cases, extremism. My first two years at university were indeed my most fervent period as a Christian, the time when I was most likely to be found at a prayer meeting, annotating and underlining passages in my Bible, witnessing earnestly to anyone who would listen or militantly striding out at a "March for Jesus". I can hardly believe now that, one 31 October, I went to a meeting to "pray against" the occult dimension of the university's Halloween parties and, had it not been for a prior engagement, would have picketed the university cinema on the evening they screened "The Last Temptation of Christ"[7]. I even considered spending my summer holidays as a missionary on the Continent, as part of the oddly named "Love Europe" crusade, travelling from country to country and reaching out to the unchurched – thank goodness (or should that be "thank God"?) I decided to spend my holidays gainfully employed in the UK instead, albeit in the quasi-spiritual atmosphere of Canterbury Cathedral, selling guidebooks, audio tours and overpriced pens and erasers bearing pictures of Chaucer's pilgrims to tourists in the gift shop and brushing up my foreign language skills.

Towards the end of my time at university, the chaplain organised a "Christian Vocations Day" to which various people in faith-related jobs were invited to talk to the students. I was, at that time, nervously looking forward to graduating and moving out into the world, but with little idea of what to do with my life, and a 'Christian' vocation was one option I was exploring, so I decided to attend. The day turned out to be interesting, not because it encouraged me to take up a Christian vocation (in fact, it effectively put me off) but because it illustrated so well the very best, and the very worst, of the broad mosaic that is Christianity today.

The best was represented by a Roman Catholic nun, who came dressed not in a habit and a wimple but in a modest, stylish trouser suit to present her work on a deprived housing estate in the West Midlands. She shared a house on this estate with two other nuns, and, together, they ministered particularly to the local children, young people and single parents. She explained how they interpreted their traditional vows of poverty, chastity and obedience for the modern age. Poverty meant for her sharing her possessions with the other nuns and opening their home at all hours of the day and night to welcome those in need – after all, who can claim to be living in poverty when they live in a developed country, have enough to eat, clothes to wear and a roof over their head? Chastity was not depriving herself of something, but rather the opportunity to have (non-sexual) relationships with a greater range of people than would have been possible had she been in an exclusive relationship with a partner. Finally, obedience meant to her not behaving selfishly, seeking to coordinate her action with that of her sister nuns, and acting in the best interests of others rather than thinking solely of herself. I warmed to this intelligent, articulate young woman who had evidently thought deeply about how to apply daunting and, some would say, old fashioned values to reflect the reality of her surroundings.

She was followed by another young woman who represented the worst of the Christian spectrum. A swivel-eyed fundamentalist, she told us how she had been travelling as a tourist in North Africa after graduation from university. As her train passed by a

Moroccan village, she had had a sudden 'insight'. "I realised," she said "that, unless I did something about it, all the people in that village, and the next, and the next, would be going to Hell!" This revelation had prompted her to hot-foot it back to Britain to take a course at an evangelical Bible college to become a missionary to the heathen. As I listened to her bigotry, I felt almost disgusted with myself that, as a card-carrying Christian, I was tacitly allying myself with such a person, that we were, in effect, playing on the same side. This was not the kind of company I wished to keep. I realised that my life and my future vocation lay elsewhere.

---

[7] Years later, I watched the *Last Temptation*, based on the novel by Cretan author Nikos Kazantzakis, and found it to be a deeply moving film in which Christ is portrayed warmly, humanely and affectionately. It courted controversy because of a scene where Jesus, hanging on the cross shortly before His death, starts to wonder what life would be like if He were able to escape from His predicament, cast off His God-given burden and lead a normal life. He imagines marrying Mary Magdalene and (this is the controversial bit) briefly, and seen from some considerable distance, making love to her. In the next scene, the two of them are shown walking along the street, hand-in-hand with a small child, presumably their common offspring. However, despite longing to settle down and marry, Jesus realises that He has a mission to perform, and the film returns to His agonies on the cross and subsequent death.

It is quite clear from the context that the director is not implying that Jesus did these things but rather that, in the agonising hours leading up to His death, He may have considered how His life could have been different. The fact that the love-making is imagined and of the orthodox variety (in other words, it is heterosexual and within marriage) was of no consequence to the hundreds of complainants who blasted the BBC when the film was shown. To them, depicting Jesus as anything other than completely asexual was blasphemous, even though, if He really was both God and man, presumably being 'man' also implies being sexual. Ascribing any sexuality to Jesus, even what could be described as 'conventional' sexuality, is the great taboo for Christians, and this absurd denial of His being a sexual person, despite the tradition of His being both human and divine, and, by extrapolation, the denial of His mother Mary's sexuality, too, has had profound repercussions on the Church's whole attitude to sex and to women which are only now being rectified, two thousand years too late.

Disillusion

Pink Floyd were wrong when, in their anthem "Another Brick in the Wall", they claimed that "We don't need no education / We don't need no thought control". Education, far from controlling your thoughts, sets them free, allowing you to rise above the assumptions and certainties of your own environment and to see the world through new eyes, question what you once took for granted and search for the truth yourself.

Although, as mentioned in the last chapter, universities can indeed become hotbeds of religious extremism, they also, by educating, sow the seeds of disillusion. It is difficult for a belief system as childish as the more fundamentalist variants of evangelical Christianity to survive the intellectual rigours of a university education. For any Christian young person growing into adulthood, the question arises as to how to reconcile the dualism that characterises their faith (God/the Devil; Heaven/Hell; angels/demons, etc.) with the growing realisation that the world is more complicated, subtle and nuanced than that. How can the attitude that blind faith in things unseen is a virtue be reconciled with the principle of rational inquiry based on believing nothing unless you have good reason to do so and the conviction that progress is made by challenging existing orthodoxy and arriving at a new consensus rather than sanctifying traditions sometimes many thousands of years old? It is also hard for those who have been surrounded by likeminded fellow students to graduate, leave the comforting university environment and pursue their faith in the very different circumstances of the real world. When I was at university, I heard a statistic that shocked me then but would not do so now – that around three quarters of Christian Union presidents at university were no longer attending church one year after graduation. After three or four years of worshipping together with your peers (both intellectually and in terms of age), the shock of attending a church in the outside world, perhaps geared more towards children, attended mainly by the elderly or the less intellectually gifted, is not to be underestimated. Add to that the shock faced by all students, religious or not, when they leave full time education after almost twenty years and have to suddenly act as economic free agents, making their own way in the world, and it is not surprising that even the most zealous Christians at university will sometimes lose their faith or at least cease to practise it after graduation.

My loss of faith was a gradual, protracted process, punctuated by sudden flashes of insight when I realised that certain aspects of what I believed were untenable. It was an emotionally grinding experience, as old certainties crumbled but no new ones arrived to take their place. I also felt very guilty about what was happening, as if my withdrawal from faith were somehow a sin, somehow my fault, as if, to use that emotionally loaded phrase from the Epistle to the Hebrews, rethinking my views would be akin to "crucifying Christ for a second time".

The principle behind a barbed fishhook or harpoon is that, in addition to the main point which facilitates entry into the body, a number of points facing the opposite direction make its extraction difficult and painful without ripping the flesh. Christianity is similar. Offering many benefits, not least eternal life, the Christianity meme enters the brain easily, but barbs pointing in the opposite direction (the guilt associated with apostasy, the concept of "crucifying Christ a second time") make it difficult to extract painlessly. It is extremely difficult to give up the certainties offered by evangelical Christianity and the fellowship of your fellow believers in exchange for the lonely, uncomfortable (but intellectually honest and ultimately liberating) truth that, *when it comes to all things God-related, we cannot know anything for certain.* Matthew Arnold captured the sense of loss as old certainties crumble in his poem "On Dover Beach",

The Sea of Faith
Was once, too, at the full, and round earth's shore
Lay like the folds of a bright girdle furl'd.
But now I only hear
Its melancholy, long, withdrawing roar,
Retreating, to the breath
Of the night-wind, down the vast edges drear
And naked shingles of the world.

The incidents that, eventually, would lead to my abandoning the faith in which I had invested so much during my teenage years, started when I was twenty years old. Of course, similar events must have happened before then, so it would perhaps be more accurate to say that, as I turned twenty, my radars for hypocrisy, inhumanity, manipulation and gullibility had become sufficiently well developed to identify anomalies which, before, would have passed me by unnoticed.

Perhaps the first of these events was a trip made by our church youth group to Leeds Castle in Kent to take part in a live broadcast of Songs of Praise led by Christian singer - song writer Graham Kendrick. Thousands of local Christians packed a field in the castle grounds, just a few hundred metres from the moat, with our backs to the medieval keep where King Henry the Eighth had once cavorted merrily with the young Anne Boleyn.

We arrived, in a state of high excitement, shortly after midday one Sunday afternoon. The plan was to rehearse the songs, most of which were already well known to the participants, during the afternoon, following which we would then be broadcast live on Songs of Praise at around six o'clock the same evening.

The rehearsals passed without a hitch, the sun shone in a cloudless blue sky, and the excitement mounted as six o'clock approached. The Songs of Praise presenter and Graham Kendrick warmed up the crowd and led us in a countdown to the live transmission.

As the allocated time arrived, and the presenter failed to give his opening speech, we started to realise that something was wrong. The presenter did not deliver his opening gambit or our cue to start the first song, we started to shuffle our feet and wonder what was happening. A minute or so later, we were told that the BBC was experiencing technical difficulties with the live broadcast, and that the viewers at home were being shown an old episode of Songs of Praise instead until the problem could be resolved. The disappointed silence that had descended over the crowd was interrupted by a member of my church breaking into song:

"I will build my church, and the gates of Hell shall not prevail against it.
And ye powers in the heavens above, bow down!
And ye powers on the Earth below, bow down!
And acknowledge that Jesus is Lord!"

The theme was taken up by the rest of crowd, and I realised that, far from singing to pass the time until the transmission was re-established, those around me really did believe that they were engaged in some kind of supernatural battle against the "powers in the heavens above ... and ... powers on the Earth below", that, at that moment, the powers of darkness were conspiring to block transmission of Songs of Praise and that we could influence the outcome of this cosmic tug-of-war by commanding them to "bow down" to Jesus. A disturbing, medieval response to a twentieth century technical glitch.

(In the event, the powers of good and the powers of darkness could be considered to have scored a one-all draw – live Songs of Praise had to be abandoned that evening, in favour of an old episode, but the Leeds Castle broadcast was shown in full the following Sunday evening. I was even able to make myself out, a small dot jigging up and down right at the back of the crowd.)

I was forced, for the first time, to consider whether I wished to belong to a faith community that believed in an ongoing Manichean cosmic struggle between good and evil, where human beings could command demons by invoking Jesus' name. An uncomfortable proposition that I was not prepared to deal with at that moment.

I remember another occasion, several years later, when I was party to a conversation between a friend and another young woman about her marital difficulties. "He asked me whether I minded him going to the pub," she began, "And I said 'No, you go'. Then, all of a sudden, the Devil said to me 'Tell him he can't!'. So I told him he couldn't go. He started sulking, and the Lord said 'Why not let him go?', but the Devil said 'No, let him stew in his own juice for a bit'...". She carried on talking in this vein for several minutes, ascribing her own mixed feelings about her husband to Jesus and the Devil whispering conflicting messages to her, rather like a character in a child's cartoon might be portrayed as having a demon on one shoulder, tempting her to do wrong, and an angel on the other, to symbolically represent wrestling with one's conscience. I hope that her church tried to gently dissuade her from dealing with her emotions in this way, but I fear that, knowing the kind of church it was, she was in fact encouraged to imagine the Devil as a real being, tempting her and plotting to wreck her marriage. I found it disturbing that, as the twentieth century drew to a close, people still seriously thought in such a way.

At around the same time, the minister of our church, a kind and gentle man who was unfortunately prone to being unduly influenced by some of the more wily members of his flock, decided that the church needed a new level of hierarchy to manage it.

Trotting out various biblical references in support, he proposed the appointment of a three "elders", who would lead the church as his personal assistants, a higher authority than the existing body of "deacons", a kind of church committee. One of the middle-aged gentlemen[8] proposed had alighted at our church some months beforehand, having attended various churches in the area over the previous years. He combined an infectious laugh and jocular over-familiarity with extreme religiosity. My parents already knew him well as they attended a Bible study group at his beautiful home with its sweeping views over the South Downs, bought not only because he liked it but because, apparently, the Lord had told him to live there. "I was reading my Bible one morning," he had told the group, "and when I reached the passage '*I will lift mine eyes unto the hills, from whence cometh my aid*' I knew that was God's way of telling me to buy this house".

A church meeting was arranged to "prayerfully consider" this change to the church's constitution. It began with the singing of choruses – warm, emotive, suggestive ones, to soften resistance and induce a feeling of oneness ("Bind us together, Lord, Bind us together…"). We then prayed in small groups, each led by a member of the church hierarchy. The prayers were of the "Your will be done" variety, but clearly an agenda that had already been decided upon was being pushed. During the ensuing discussion, I commented that a decision appeared to have already been made on our behalf and that our role, as a church meeting, was apparently just to rubber stamp it. Perish the thought, countered the minister – no decision had yet been taken, and the views of the members would be binding. When it came to the point for a decision to be made, evidently anticipating little resistance, the minister said "Well, I think we know in which way the Holy Spirit is leading us…".

He looked surprised when my father piped up, saying "I think we should vote on this". I had just expressed my agreement when the wife of the gentleman proposed as an elder requested permission to address the meeting. "I know that appointing a body of elders is the right thing for this church," she declared, "because the Lord told me so himself!". At that, all resistance crumbled – after all, if the Lord had decided already, who were we mere mortals to disagree? Playing the "I had a vision/word from the Lord" card never failed.

Until that day, I had entertained the rather naïve view that the Church was Christ's representative on Earth, His body, or some such vicarious organisation, standing in for the Risen Jesus until His return. But, at that church meeting, I was brought face-to-face with the reality that *the Church is, in essence, an instrument of control*. As small children at Sunday School, we were made to sing the hymn "Trust and Obey", by John H. Sammis, which makes the position abundantly clear: "Trust and obey, for there's no other way, to be happy in Jesus, but to *trust and obey*!". In other words, do as you are told, and keep your mouth shut.

The church has always existed primarily to control the way people think, so as to control their behaviour and combat unorthodox thinking. This is not necessarily a criticism – after all, any campaigning organisation, from Amnesty International to the RSPCA, exists to make people think along certain lines so that this will have an impact on their behaviour and, ultimately, change society. Yet so many church-going Christians never give a moment's thought to the way they are submitting their will and their intellect to an extremely powerful organisation, and how this makes them vulnerable to being manipulated.

* * *

Some months later, another church meeting was held to discuss the thorny issue of Des and Emily's applications for church membership. It was university term time, so I did not attend, but my parents recounted the meeting to me during my next visit home. The situation to be discussed was that Emily, a single woman in her thirties, had started attending the church. Pleased with the welcome she received, she persuaded her lodger, Des, a single man of similar years, to attend with her. Not only did they find that they enjoyed attending church together, but they were increasingly enjoying each other's company as well and were soon engaged to be married. They asked the minister of the church to marry them and also applied for full church membership. The difficulty was that they were still sharing the same house, and the question put to the church was whether it would be unseemly for two church members of the opposite sex, in a relationship with each other, to share the same address even though they were not married. Apparently, the couple had assured the minister that they were not sleeping together, having decided, quaintly, to 'save themselves' for their wedding day, and it was accepted that they were telling the truth, but the church was asked to debate whether granting their applications would give the *appearance* of moral laxity even though it was accepted that their situation was perfectly above-board. After a brief debate, it was decided that their applications for membership should be refused until such time as their domestic arrangements had been sorted out.

This story disturbed me for several reasons. Firstly, I was myself a young adult looking forward to the possibility of future relationships and, ultimately, marriage and was appalled that, as I was also a church member, my future decisions in this area could form the subject of church meetings. By what right did the church presume to pass judgements on consenting adults' relationships with each other? Did membership of a church mean that it possessed a veto over certain areas of my private life? I had already decided at this stage that the church's disapproval of cohabitation before marriage was wrong and that I would, of course, want to live with any potential marriage partner before walking up the aisle, and I was not about to let church membership dictate how I lived.

Moreover, the fact that this couple had sworn that they were not sleeping together but were still barred from membership because of *appearances* was a revelation to me. The underlying philosophy was so hypocritical that I wanted nothing to do with it. Walter Mitty-like, I fantasised about having been at the church meeting and having taken a lone stand to denounce the rest of the members for being such hypocrites, but the issue was not raised again at subsequent meetings I attended. The couple apparently took the judgement of the church magnanimously, deferred their applications, were married and then successfully reapplied and, as far as I know, lived happily ever after. But I was enraged on their behalf.

I came to realise, guiltily, that I didn't *like* certain aspects of Jesus' character much, an odd concept perhaps, given that, as a Christian, you are supposed to have a personal relationship with Jesus and *love* Him, just as He loves you ("Jesus we love you, we worship and adore you. Glorify your name through all the Earth…", as the hymn goes). Perhaps, if I had met Him in the flesh, I would have liked Him. Perhaps He would have worked His magic on me, bowled me over with that charisma that worked on His disciples. Yet the Jesus of, for example, Luke's Gospel, Chapter 10 verses 10 to 15, is not portrayed as being particularly likeable, as He curses various villages for not accepting His message, issuing violent threats that the punishment meted out to them on Judgement Day will be more severe than that which destroyed Sodom[9]. This was the person whose example I sought to follow, a supposedly sinless man, threatening individual men, women and children with perdition for little more than their natural scepticism. How could that be reconciled with gentle Jesus, meek and mild, laying down His life for the world?

It is much easier to imagine being friends with St John's Christ, or St Paul's version of Christ in his epistles. But which version of Jesus is the most accurate? Would the real Jesus please stand up? Yet again, we run into the unavoidable problem that, because He wrote down nothing Himself, as far as we know, the portrayal of Jesus in the New Testament is inevitably seen through the distorted glass of the hopes, fears, prejudices and beliefs of the Gospel writers themselves.

Little by little, the faith of my teenage years was being eroded as youthful idealism collided with reality, and the rightwing, socially conservative Christianity I had once accepted collided with a new founded interest in human and civil rights. Some evangelical Christians apparently manage to compartmentalise their minds so that they can accept that, in everyday life, discrimination on the grounds of religious belief is wrong while continuing to believe simultaneously in a righteous and benevolent God who damns non-believers. How else can an educated Christian satisfy the inherent contradictions between a literal interpretation of the

Scriptures and the evident evil of discrimination? As a Christian friend of mine tellingly put it, "I've got nothing against gay people. I've got lots of gay friends, but it says in the Bible that it's wrong". But I could not countenance that level of hypocrisy in my own beliefs. For me, either discrimination against people on the grounds of religious belief was wrong, in which case a benevolent God would surely agree and act accordingly, or, in the unlikely event that God sent unbelievers to Hell, any discrimination against people of other faiths here on Earth would be justified as merely a reflection of the divine order and a warning of things to come.

For a short period, I managed to keep the warring world views at bay. An Amnesty International member, I would on Sunday afternoons conscientiously write polite letters of protest to ruthless dictators requesting the release of prisoner of consciences whose only 'crime' had been their unorthodox religious beliefs, having, that morning, listened without protest (and therefore lent my tacit agreement) to a sermon urging us to evangelise our town to save our friends and neighbours from eternal damnation.

How can any intelligent, 21st-century person still believe in the concept of Hell, except perhaps as a symbol of alienation from God and fellowship with other people? Of the many memes (to borrow Richard Dawkin's term) to have developed and successfully reproduced in western thought, the Hell meme must be one of the nastiest, but also one of the most useful, hence its success. The Church would have you believe that its historic success has been due to the attractiveness of the Christian Gospel, the reasoning being that Christianity must be true because, over the last two thousand years, many millions of people have come to know the love of Christ and the reality of a relationship with

Him for themselves, and that so many people cannot be wrong. Perhaps there is an element of truth in this argument, but the Roman Catholic Church's hegemony in European political and cultural life from the fall of the Roman Empire in the fifth century AD until the Reformation some one thousand years later can be attributed in no small part to the terror of Hell it spread throughout Christendom. Thousands of miles were travelled on foot by pilgrims, majestic cathedrals were constructed stone-by-stone (over several generations, with many individual craftsmen never living to see their work complete), pietas were hewn from rough marble, ceilings were painted with intricate frescos by people who believed that, by contributing in their own way to the glory of the Church, they would save themselves from hellfire (or at least shorten their stay in Purgatory). From Dante's *Divine Comedy* to Michelangelo's *Last Judgement*, the art and literature of the Middle Ages testify to the extent that, through its use of terror, the Church exercised complete control over individual minds and thus over societies as a whole.

In any other walk of life, threatening people with violence unless they behave in certain ways would be a criminal offence, but evangelical Christians are free to threaten unbelievers with the fiery pit unless they open their hearts to Jesus with impunity. Apart from the psychological damage and mental anguish inflicted by this nastiest of concepts throughout the ages, its usefulness in shoring up the use of torture even today should not be underestimated. After all, what is the point of campaigning for an end to torture throughout the world, if, on a cosmic scale, God is Torturer-in-Chief, busy creating new human beings at the rate of hundreds of millions every year in the certainty that the majority of them, some seventy years later, will be consigned to

Hell (for ever? until they have paid off their sins in Purgatory, if you are a Roman Catholic? until the Day of Judgement when Christ will give them a last chance? Thinking seriously about questions this absurd is like wondering how many angels can dance on the head of a pin[10]). If torture is condoned by the Almighty, and is in fact a integral part of how the cosmos is arranged, then why not practise it here on Earth? It is surely no coincidence that the United States, the home of evangelical Christianity, where belief in Hell is greater than in any other country of the developed world, runs Guantanamo Bay, is responsible for "extraordinary rendition" of terrorist suspects to countries where torture is practised and has a president and vice-president who, *de facto*, support torture-lite. There is a clear thread running from belief in torture in the afterlife to the practice of torture here on Earth.

The last Sunday of my regular church-going years, I was twenty two years old and had recently graduated from university. I had attended the evening service, following which a group of young people went to the minister's house for a youth group meeting, led not by the minister himself but by a motley crew of youth leaders whose qualifications for the job seemed to be that they were slightly older than the rest of us. The theme of this particular fun-packed evening was what happens to you when you die if you are not a Christian. The answer, it transpired (unsurprisingly), was that your soul fries for eternity. But how about children who are not yet old enough to decide for themselves what they believe? Perhaps they are granted Heaven by default. Up until what age? And the mentally deficient, does a get-out clause apply to them too? How about those whose Alzheimer's or dementia means that they do not have the intellectual ability to make a decision for Christ as their life nears its end but might otherwise have done so had their mind been active? As the eternal fates of these categories of unfortunates was discussed, it seemed to me that I was attending a sitting of the Spanish Inquisition, though perhaps marginally less liberal. In a similar way to St Paul who, on the Road to Damascus, had a life-changing conversion experience, that evening was, for me, a life-changing *deconversion* experience. I did not cover myself with glory that day. I should have spoken out, or at least walked out to demonstrate my opposition, but instead I sat through the ghoulish meeting, and my main emotion was one of shame, for acquiescing without complaint, for standing by whilst young teenagers were fed poisonous nonsense that could only damage their mental health (which, let's face it, is often fairly vulnerable at that age). Profoundly upset, I returned home, and my regular church-going life was over.

Shortly after that, I left university and then left home and, over the next few years, attended church sporadically, when visiting my parents for instance, but, overall, not more than three or four times a year. The situation was exacerbated by regularly moving as my employment situation changed and, by the time I had settled in one place again, the Sunday church-going habit had been definitively broken.

That is not to say that I did not think about Christianity any more. On the contrary, I was often wracked by fears as my intellect tore me in two directions. On the one hand, the more I learnt about the world, the less I believed the Christianity I had been taught. On the other, I preferred not to think too deeply about the doctrines that were slowly slipping from my grasp, on the basis that, if I hadn't actively rejected them, I still counted as a Christian. Sitting on the fence, keeping a foothold in both camps, not thinking about or questioning the historical truth of the resurrection, but still kind of believing it on Easter Sunday, was a far more comfortable option than deciding, once and for all, that I did not believe and living with the consequences. Why worry about the divinity of Christ, and therefore whether you still count as a Christian if you deny it, when you can just push the issues to one side and stop thinking about them? After more than a decade as a Christian, the idea of *being a non-Christian* was frightening.

I still referred to myself as a Christian when asked, although by the time I stopped attending church altogether my answers must have lacked authenticity. I went out for a short time with an intense young woman who attended a Pentecostal church. Mindful of the Church's teaching on "unequal yoking" between believers and non-believers, she would surreptitiously quiz me about my beliefs by dropping apparently off-the-cuff comments ("Look at that lovely rainbow. Isn't it wonderful how God made it a symbol of His covenant to Noah not to send another flood!") and then waiting for my response. I evidently did not provide the answers for which she was looking, as she ended the relationship after two months, and I later found out, via a mutual friend, that she had categorised me as "not Christian enough". I didn't take offence but considered it to be fair comment.

---

[8] In all the churches I attended, no woman was ever placed in a position of authority over men. The highest position to which they could aspire was that of Sunday School superintendent, a role which few men seemed to want. Even at the height of Mrs Thatcher's premiership, around 1987, before her authority started to ebb away, we were still being told by men in church, in all seriousness, that women were not created by God to be leaders.

9 Gospel of Luke, Chapter 10: [10]But when you enter a town and are not welcomed, go into its streets and say, [11]'Even the dust of your town that sticks to our feet we wipe off against you. Yet be sure of this: The kingdom of God is near.' [12]I tell you, it will be more bearable on that day for Sodom than for that town. [13]"Woe to you, Korazin! Woe to you, Bethsaida! For if the miracles that were performed in you had been performed in Tyre and Sidon, they would have repented long ago, sitting in sackcloth and ashes. [14]But it will be more bearable for Tyre and Sidon at the judgment than for you. [15]And you, Capernaum, will you be lifted up to the skies? No, you will go down to the depths. {NIV).

10 In similar vein, Pope Benedict recently announced that, henceforth, the idea of Limbo as a resting place for the souls of unbaptised infants was to be abolished. This announcement was treated as a serious piece of news by the media, but surely it is as ridiculous as Walt Disney announcing, poker-faced that , from now on, there will only be six dwarfs, not seven.

Whither the Church in the 21st century?

Where is the Church to go now, in twenty-first century Britain? How can it reconnect with those who could represent its future: young, educated people? To ask the question from another angle, which aspects of the Church are most likely to alienate young, educated people? Perhaps I could make a few suggestions.

Firstly, the Church should *drop the concept of victimless sin*. When I was a child at Sunday School, I was told that sin was "going your own way, rather than God's way", in other words, showing independence of mind rather than conforming to the Church's rules. Under this definition, God's rules have been dictated from on high, have been supernaturally revealed and are to be found in the Bible. These rules are unchanging and have to be followed because they are God's, and He knows best. Deviation from them is called sin, counts as an act of rebellion against the divine order, and alienates the sinner from God's presence. It is because of this sin-induced alienation from God that Christ had to come into the world and die a sacrificial death on the cross to bring us back into communion with Him.

This is an erroneous definition of sin for many reasons. Firstly, unlike in our modern societies, where differences in lifestyle are tolerated and increasingly welcomed, a tribe wandering the desert in Biblical times had to ensure that every member knew his or her place and acted accordingly, for any lack of internal discipline made the tribe more vulnerable to attack from outside. In the absence of any international organisations such as the United Nations or the Red Cross, or accepted standards relating to how war should be waged (such as the Geneva Conventions), the only law governing how nations behaved towards each other in Old Testament times was dog-eat-dog. To survive, tribal or national units had to act ruthlessly to obliterate their enemies and ensure discipline and internal hegemony of behaviour and belief within their own tribal group. The ancient Israelites at the time of Moses were wandering the desert, competing with many other tribes for scarce resources, in the full knowledge that, if attacked and defeated by an enemy tribe, they would probably be annihilated (which is, in fact, exactly what the Isrealites did to many of their enemies – the Book of Joshua, chapter 6, verses 20 and 21 demonstrates the ruthlessness of the Israelites and their likely fate had they been defeated by an enemy nation[11]). In such circumstances, discipline was everything, and it was vitally important for everyone to believe and act in the same way. Being a moral person was not so much about respecting the freedom of others and showing consideration to them as about conforming rigidly with the group. (This emphasis on discipline and conformity of belief has been a defining characteristic of Judeo-Christianity ever since, and is reflected still today in some evangelicals' belief that those who believe the wrong things about God and the supernatural will end up in Hell, regardless of how much good they might have done in the world during their life.)

Covering everything from clean and unclean animals to how to treat your slaves and how men should behave the day after they have a nocturnal emission or how women should conduct themselves during their monthly periods, the rules set out by Moses were highly culturally specific and, even if they made sense when they were first enacted, do not do so now. Even the most literalist Christian ignores the vast majority of the injunctions in the books of the Bible known as the Pentateuch (Genesis, Exodus, Leviticus, Numbers and Deuteronomy), although he would probably brook no dissent when it comes to the universal applicability of his pet rules, whether they concern keeping the Sabbath holy or sexual morality.

The guiding principle of behaviour in modern liberal democracies, however, is that people should be free to live as they wish, until the point is reached where their actions start to impinge upon the freedom of others. At the point where that occurs, a law is created, the breaking of which makes the offender liable to civil or criminal sanctions. Of course, this abstract principle can be difficult to apply in practice, and disputes often arise about exactly where one person's freedoms become a nuisance to others (does my wish to smoke a cigarette after dinner in a restaurant impinge upon other diners' rights to enjoy a smoke-free meal, or the waiter's right to work in a smoke-free environment, for example?), but it is a generally accepted principle of western societies.

The orthodox Christian view of sin and law, on the other hand, could not be more different. Far from acting as a kind of referee between free individuals trying to pursue incompatible activities, the law is considered to have been laid down by God in the Old and New Testaments (so between around 3500 and 2000 years ago) through a process of inerrant divine revelation. Moses ascended Mount Sinai, met with God and had the Law dictated to him – in a trance, he copied it down. It does not exist to protect human freedom but to ensure that the universe is governed in accordance with God's wishes. Particular actions are wrong, evil, sinful (describe them as you will) not because they hurt others or damage their freedom *per se*, but rather because they do not meet the perfect standards that God has set. That is enough to constitute an offence. No victim is required, no demonstrable hurt or damage to another person (or, by extension, another sentient being, such as an animal). Two elderly lesbians cohabiting faithfully for years, their loving relationship affecting no one else, are nevertheless 'living in sin' (to use that dreadful phrase that, until recently, was mainly reserved for cohabiting heterosexual couples) because they are allegedly breaking "God's Law". Yet, in any sensible definition, the concept of a 'victimless sin' is an oxymoron, a contradiction in terms, the equivalent of a 'curved line' or a 'four-sided triangle'. A victim, whether individual or collective, is a precondition for a sinful/wicked/immoral act having been committed.

The Church also needs to update its position regarding the *concept of truth*, specifically the relative merits of "revealed" truth (absolute and eternal truth supposedly given by God to man supernaturally and in full, for example the delivery of the Ten Commandments and the Old Testament laws to Moses on Mount Sinai) and "observed" or scientific truth.

The idea of revealed truth, the idea that God spoke definitively to human beings at some point several thousand years ago and that any developments in human thought since that time are automatically of lesser value, has long been due for an overhaul. It goes against the grain of how we find out about the world from our earliest years when, like my two-year-old son, we push at the boundaries of the world we know and constantly test new discoveries. A toddler, like a scientist, makes hypotheses about how the world works, tests them and then confirms or revises these hypotheses. The scientific method of hypothesis followed by experiment and adjustment is a powerful way of finding the truth, the most powerful yet devised. Science, far from being "just one way of looking at the world", as some religious people would have you believe, is nothing less than the search for truth. For example, if an astronomer devises a hypothesis to explain how the heavenly bodies move in relation to each other and, on the basis of this hypothesis, predicts that an eclipse of the moon will be visible at a specific time at a specific place on the Earth's surface, and this prediction proves to be correct, his theory has been proved true. If he predicts further eclipses, and the times and dates he gives also prove accurate, the truth of his theory is confirmed, for ever. We can confidently predict that our current understanding of how the moon orbits the earth and how the planets orbit the sun is true and will remain true for ever. It may be tinkered with, but its essence will never be replaced by any other theory. All previous theories of how the celestial bodies interacted, from the flat-earth theory to the Greek mythological idea of the Earth being carried through the void on the shoulders of the giant Atlas, have been proved definitively to be wrong. They were not alternative descriptions of reality. They were untrue. Full stop. That is truth.

The idea that, for example, angels exist as a kind of intermediate step between God and mortal human beings, that their role in Heaven is to praise God unceasingly and to act as God's messengers and that they watch over and protect us while we sleep is not *truth* in the same way (which is not the same thing as saying that it is not *true*). It is impossible to design or carry out an experiment to prove or disprove that angels exist or to observe their movements and behaviour. Their existence cannot therefore be regarded as truth in the same way as a scientifically confirmed fact, and cannot even be compared to such a fact. It is not good enough to say that all beliefs, however way-out or lacking in evidence, should be accorded the same dignity, that belief in angels should be given the same weight as belief in, say, gravity or the Big Bang, as one is a belief based on ancient myths and the other on scientific observation, and the two are not comparable. It is simply not the case that science and religion are two different, but equally valid, ways of looking at the world.

Related to the church's position on revealed truth is its position on myth. One shared characteristic of all human beings and societies is that they like to understand how and why things happen, and, if you live in a pre-scientific society, the only way to construct meaningful answers to the question of why things happen is to invent mythological stories. Why does the sun rise in the East and set in the West? Because Apollo the sun god draws it across the sky in his chariot. What happens when a ship reaches the horizon? It falls off the edge into the void. Why does a particular man behave oddly and shout at strangers in the street? Because he's possessed by a demon. Why is that woman lame? Because her sins have not yet been forgiven. And so on.

In the absence of any other knowledge, all these pre-scientific answers to difficult questions are logical and understandable. If they are the best answers available, and everyone else shares them, then why not believe them? But if you are fortunate enough to live, as we do, in an enlightened age when we understand why the sun moves across the sky, and that the Earth is round, not flat, and that paralysis has a physical, not a spiritual cause, then it is nothing short of perverse to carry on believing the myths developed by ancient peoples *despite all the evidence to the contrary.* A man in first century Palestine who believed that demons could be ordered out of human beings and sent to live in a herd of pigs was acting logically in the absence of any better medical explanation, whereas anyone who believes that now is perversely and obstinately clinging to what he knows to be untrue. Claiming, as fundamentalist Christians do, that a particular myth is recounted in the Bible, which means it must be true, is wilful stupidity. Pre-scientific people had an excuse – we don't.

Thirdly, the evangelical wing of the Church, when it tries to frighten people into becoming Christians by invoking the fear of Hell, finds itself in the unpleasant position of creating one of the only contexts where demanding with menaces is not illegal. In almost every other situation, if I were to threaten you with violence in order to persuade you to follow a particular course of action, I would be committing a criminal offence, but the law makes an exception for me if I try to urge you to "give your heart to Jesus" on pain of a thorough roasting in the hereafter.

As William C. Easttom puts it "Conservative Christian theologians teach that if you make the wrong choice and believe the wrong thing, you will be tortured for eternity in hell. That's not a choice, it's more like a man telling his girlfriend, do what you wish, but if you choose to leave me, I will track you down and blow your brains out. When a man says this we call him a psychopath."

There is little moral difference between a protection racket, where, for example, a shopkeeper is forced to pay a certain amount each month to criminals to "protect" his property against vandalism by persons unknown, and the spiritual protection racket of evangelical Christianity, where churches gain more members and grow rich by skilfully holding out the threat of eternal punishment for the "unsaved".

In the unlikely event that evangelicals were correct about Hell for unbelievers, this would put humanity in the interesting position of having evolved to become more ethical than its creator. The United Nations Declaration of Human Rights of 1948 states unequivocally that "No one shall be subjected to torture or to cruel, inhuman or degrading treatment or punishment" (Article 5) and that "Everyone has the right to freedom of thought, conscience and religion; this right includes freedom to change his religion or belief, and freedom, either alone or in community with others and in public or private, to manifest his religion or belief in teaching, practice, worship and observance" (Article 18). We, as human beings, have created in the UN Declaration of Human Rights a moral code superior to that set out – allegedly by God Himself – in the Bible, and it would therefore be our duty as the most intelligent life forms in the universe (as far as we know), to tell God that His arrangements are cruel, arbitrary and completely unacceptable. Preaching from the pulpit that the torture of people who believe differently is not only morally right but is God's will and plan for the universe is inexcusable and cowardly.

* * *

When you consider that the Church today is also one of the last bastions of explicit sexism and homophobia, that the clergy is one of the last professions left where you can legally be dismissed because you are gay or refused for promotion because you are a woman, it is a wonder that anyone would wish to keep such unsavoury company. That is perhaps the biggest problem facing the Church – to survive and grow, it needs to recruit sufficient numbers of young, preferably educated people, but with its covert threats of extreme violence in the hereafter and its institutionalised sexism and homophobia it is increasing distasteful to most morally aware people, who regard with abhorrence any organisation governed by views of that kind. Why would anyone wish to join, and thus tacitly show their approval of, an organisation where women are permitted to be priests but are refused promotion to any higher office? Why would they wish to join an organisation tearing itself apart over the rights and wrongs of the appointment of the Rt Rev Katharine Jefferts Schoria as Bishop of Nevada, the first woman bishop in the Anglican Community, when, all over the world, women are reaching the pinnacles of political leadership and, in certain cases are performing better in their role than their male predecessors? If Hillary Clinton wins her bid for the White House in 2008 and becomes President of the United States, which appears to be a real possibility at the time of writing, how will the church possibly be able to defend its position that women can join the lower ranks of the clergy but never become bishops, because God did not create women to be leaders?

The doctrine of the atonement, the idea that Christ came to Earth where He was killed to pay for our sins, to save us from the righteous wrath of God, is just one area of the Church's teaching that seems anachronistic in the 21st century. Dr Giles Fraser, Vicar of Putney, writing in The Guardian on 10 January 2007, described the evangelical Christian interpretation of the atonement in these terms:

" *Human beings are wicked and can only make it to heaven if they are punished for their sin, thus righting the scales of justice and wiping clean the slate. The problem is, human wickedness is so deep that the required punishment would be too much for us to bear. So Christ offers to take our place, accepting our punishment in the form of an excruciating crucifixion. It's the story of salvation, as read by the religious right. All sin must be paid for with pain... The technical term for this theology is penal substitution. It is, among other things, the reason so many conservative Christians ... support the death penalty – wickedness must be paid for with blood.*"

Historically, cultures located as far apart as the Mexican Aztecs and Nepalese Hindus have offered animal sacrifices (with the former also known for their penchant for human sacrifice). Animal sacrifice still played an important part in the religious life of first-century Jews, and it is evident from a critical reading of the New Testament that the doctrine of sacrifice was applied to the death of Christ many years later so as to try to make sense of this particularly traumatic event. St. Paul, an educated first century AD Jew, would have been familiar with the Old Testament stories portraying *Yahweh*, or Jehovah, as a jealous and wrathful god who needed to be placated on a regular basis by animal sacrifices – indeed, one of the first episodes in the Old Testament, in Genesis 4, has Abel bringing an animal sacrifice to the Lord (which was more acceptable to Him than Cain's vegetarian offering), and this leitmotif was continued with Abraham's near-sacrifice of his son Isaac and the first Passover shortly before the Israelites fled Egypt. Reflecting on a senseless act of violence against Jesus, a non-violent man, St. Paul interpreted his crucifixion in sacrificial terms, with Christ taking the place of the lamb, the scapegoat, killed and offered vicariously to placate a vengeful God. As he writes in the third Chapter of the Letter to the Romans "For all have sinned and fall short of the glory of God, and are justified freely by his grace through the redemption that came by Christ Jesus. God presented him as a sacrifice of atonement…". It is from this doctrine of sacrifice that Christianity takes its blood metaphors, the "blood that cleanses me" in the words of the song. Just as the blood of an animal sacrificed to God was smeared on the doorpost of the Israelites' homes shortly before their flight from Egypt, so that the angel on a mission to kill the eldest son of each Egyptian household would pass over them, so Christ's blood is supposed to divert God's wrath away from us. But is Christianity's obsession with blood imagery still helpful today as a symbol of a supposedly loving and beautiful act of grace and forgiveness?

A cartoon which particularly amused me on the website ex-christian.net depicted a man standing before the Throne of God pleading "But you died for me...!". God, clearly nonplussed, replies "Now, let me get this straight... I became myself so as to kill myself so I could placate myself. *But I'm the one who makes the rules!*" Just as the concept of killing dumb animals to mollify wrathful deities is completely alien to our society, so the idea that God, who makes the rules, had to become a human being *specifically in order to die in order to assuage his own anger* because human beings, despite being His creation, did not turn out as He intended them to, is difficult to accept. Any human father who tried to kill himself in order to make amends to himself for his own son's faults would be dragged off by the men in white coats, so why does the Church continue to ascribe conduct of this kind to God?

In his guide to recognising sloppy logic "Bad Thoughts", philosopher Jamie Whyte describes the Hitler fallacy, a sloppy, but surprisingly effective way of winning an argument. In essence, the strategy involves pretending to listen to your opponent's argument and then countering with the comment that "I'm sure Hitler would have agreed!", implying that, if Adolf thought it, it must surely be wrong. This is, of course, a totally specious argument – Hitler had many opinions on a multitude of matters, some of which were obscene or just plain wrong, but many of which would have been correct. Berlin is still a city in Germany, even though Hitler would doubtless have agreed.

You believe in the benefits of genetic engineering to tackle inherited diseases? Hitler would have agreed with you. You're a German language activist campaigning to stem the flood of English words entering German usage and the trend amongst politicians, the media and advertisers to use inappropriate English in a mistaken attempt to look cool? Hitler would have been proud! You think that animal rights are as important as human rights? So did Hitler! In each of these cases, the issue of whether or not Hitler would have agreed is completely irrelevant. All are important questions meriting serious discussion, but quoting Hitler to knock the wind out of your opponent's sails is a poor substitute for reasoned argument.

The mirror image of the Hitler fallacy is the "Bible fallacy" and its offspring, the "Jesus fallacy". Rather than stating that "Hitler would have agreed", as a *coup de grace* to kill off your opponent's argument, this strategy consists of claiming that "Jesus said…" as a way of elevating your own argument into the realms of everlasting truth. The point that we do not actually know with any certainty what "Jesus said…" has already been dealt with earlier on in this book, but, even if you were absolutely sure of Jesus' views on a particular matter, the fact that Jesus thought such a thing does not mean that you have automatically won the argument. Jesus, as a poor first-century Galilean with little formal education to speak of, would have believed all manner of things which we now know to be untrue. It is naïve to think that, in a society which generally believed the world to be flat and the sun and stars to revolve around it, Jesus would have believed any different. He certainly believed in demon possession as the cause of mental and even physical illness, for instance, and many of the miracles attributed to him involve casting out evil spirits. Whatever the exact nature of

His relationship with God, Jesus' beliefs would have been almost exclusively a reflection of those of his peers, and He would have erred in His thinking as they did. To refuse to discuss a matter that is crying out for intelligent debate on the basis that, two thousand years ago, in a pre-scientific age, "Jesus said X" or, three thousand years ago, in a nomadic society even more alien to our own, "Moses said Y" is to commit the Hitler fallacy in reverse.

* * *

The mind-body dualism of evangelical Christianity, the idea of a 'ghost in the machine' looks increasingly shaky in the light of new research into the brain and the nature of consciousness. The Bible writers clearly believed in the duality of body and spirit, an idea articulated by Plato and, much later, Christianised by St Thomas Aquinas. Human beings, according to this tradition, comprise a physical part made of flesh, blood, bones and brain, and a non-physical or spiritual self, the soul, the seat of consciousness. The soul is placed in the body at conception (hence evangelical Christians' hatred of abortion or, indeed, any research on embryos), coexists with the body during a person's life and is then released from the body at death to be judged and proceed to the afterlife. It is at the level of the soul that human beings interact with God – when you invite Jesus 'into your heart', He enters your soul through the Holy Spirit. My mother's analogy of a dead body as a kind of empty box of chocolates reflects this idea of mind-body dualism.

Modern brain research, however, suggests that what we call consciousness exists as a physical phenomenon in the brain, that our personalities are largely determined physically by our genetic make-up, and that feelings, emotions and mental disorders such as depression or even addictive behaviour are mainly the result of chemical and physical changes in the brain. One of the most potent pieces of evidence in favour of this view is the extreme changes in behaviour that can be observed in people who have suffered brain injuries. In such cases, it is obviously the injured brain, rather than an independent spirit or soul, which is acting differently.

If human beings do not have both a body and a soul, but just a body which includes the brain, the seat of feelings, consciousness and behaviour, as is starting to appear to be the case, then several aspects of Christianity become untenable, and the whole edifice starts to crumble, the most obvious being the concept of life after death, which becomes a complete oxymoron (if it were ever otherwise). The personality, if it is a function of the brain rather than a soul or spirit residing somewhere within it, must cease to exist at the moment of brain death rather than continuing to live in a shadowy, disembodied form in an afterlife. Moreover, if the personality, what we think of as the essence of a person, is composed even in part of genetic hardware influenced by chemical software, then the idea of free will and, consequently, sin and judgement no longer stands up to examination. The evangelical idea of Jesus Christ entering your heart or soul upon conversion and residing there through his Holy Spirit also collapses if the soul does not exist. Most significantly, the whole concept of the incarnation of Christ, with a young virgin conceiving not as a result of sexual intercourse but through the supernatural intervention of God Himself and giving birth to an ephemeral human body possessed of the eternal soul of God, starts to crumble. The majestic opening chapter of St John's Gospel – "In the beginning was the Word… and the Word became flesh and dwelt among us, full of grace and truth" – makes sense only in the context of mind-body dualism.

---

[11] Joshua, chapter 6: 20 When the trumpets sounded, the people shouted, and at the sound of the trumpet, when the people gave a loud shout, the wall collapsed; so every man charged straight in, and they took the city. 21 They devoted the city to the LORD and *destroyed with the sword every living thing in it—men and women, young and old*, cattle, sheep and donkeys. (My italics. New International Version.)

The Recovering Christian

The website www.exchristian.net is packed with testimonies from people who have seen the error of their ways and converted… from Christianity (back) to atheism or humanism. Many of them come from much more extreme backgrounds than my own evangelical Christian one, but all are united in their new-found sense of freedom, as if a vast weight has been lifted from their shoulders. Yet can you ever be an "ex-" Christian? I prefer the term "recovering Christian". In much the same way as an alcoholic who has successfully tackled his addiction might refer to himself as a "recovering" alcoholic rather than a "former" alcoholic, on the basis that excessive exposure to drink could trigger a relapse, so, as a recovering Christian, I realise that I will never be completely free of the faith of my childhood and young adulthood. I still feel a certain amount of nostalgia for those Sunday mornings when

I would rise full of anticipation, looking forward to the coming church service, the comfort of being part of a large community of people who cared for you (and, in most cases, I think their care was genuine), the spine-tingling experience of singing a rousing hymn in unison with several hundred other voices. All these sensations flood back on the rare occasions when I attend church, normally to be followed by disillusion when the minister starts his sermon. The fact that I decided to write an autobiography concentrating on this aspect of my life, to the exclusion of all the other aspects of it, shows the hold that evangelical Christianity still has on me fifteen years after I stopped attending church regularly, my fascination with the church and Christian spirituality. I am writing these very lines in mid December, listening to and enjoying Christmas carols on the radio. In fact, Christmas is the one time of the year when I yearn to slip back into church, any church, for a candle-lit carol service, sit in a pew on the back row, in case I am noticed or, worse, drawn into conversation, and sing joyfully along with the choir and congregation to "It came upon a midnight clear" or "As with gladness men of old".

Could I describe myself as a Christian now? Only if the term is used in its most elastic sense. Perhaps a "deist" would be the best description, according to the definition in the Collins English Dictionary: "[one who believes] in the existence of Good based solely on natural reason, without reference to revelation". In other words, I can see in the design of the physical and chemical laws of the universe, upon which all life and non-living matter is based, evidence of a divine hand which originally created and now upholds the universe, but I find it increasingly difficult to believe in a God who intervenes in a personal way in human lives, who can be prompted to act in certain ways by our prayers or who keeps a record of the thoughts, feelings and actions of all the six billion human beings currently on this planet (not to mention any other intelligent life elsewhere in the universe), like a celestial accountant ascribing transactions to one side or the other of a profit-and-loss account.

Conduct this thought experiment with me: at Sunday school one day when I was around thirteen years old, our teacher asked us to pray for her as she and her husband were planning to move to a new town and, that afternoon, were taking their family to look at a house they wanted to buy. We were encouraged to pray that this house would be the right one for them. But exactly how could God have intervened in that situation? Could He have changed the features of the property to make them more appropriate? Clearly not. A four-bedroom house benefiting from an elevated position, central heating and full double glazing throughout will remain so, however much you pray about it. Perhaps God could change the buyer's opinion of it, but why would you, as a buyer, pray for that? Or perhaps He could work a little divine magic on the seller's side – persuading the seller to drop the price, say, or discouraging other interested parties. Let us assume that God had intervened supernaturally to make the seller favour our Sunday school teacher, as a consequence of our prayers, to the disadvantage of several other potential buyers also interested in the same property. Think about how many lives would have been affected by God's intervention: the buyer's and her family's, the families of the other buyers who would have to move elsewhere, the lives of any other people with whom they came into contact but would never have known had God not intervened. For example, divine intervention could have meant that the children of my Sunday school teacher would have moved into a particular house, meaning that they would have attended a particular school where they might have met their future spouse, a person they would never have met otherwise, and thus given birth to children that would never otherwise have existed. So one act of divine intervention could potentially have affected many different families over several generations, sending out waves of repercussions, in much the same way as a pebble thrown into a pond sends out ripples in all directions over a much larger surface area than that of the pebble. And this example relates to secular Britain, where, in most cases, it is assumed that God does *not* intervene. Now imagine the situation somewhere in the American Bible Belt, where a majority of people consider themselves to be 'born again' and pray regularly to ask God to intervene in the details of their lives. Imagine the complex web of repercussions as God tries to answer everyone's prayers to everyone's own advantage. It is clear that, in such a situation, God would be directing the whole show, with little or no room left for any human free will.

The potential repercussions of just one act of divine intervention mean that, assuming He exists, God either does not intervene in the human story, in which case we have free will and are responsible for our actions, or, if He does intervene, we might as well lie back and go with the flow, content to leave Him to direct events, but the orthodox Christian view of a God who intervenes in human life as a response to prayer but leaves us to act and respond freely is untenable.

For many people, the tsunami of Boxing Day 2004 challenged their faith – for me, it was just another nail in its coffin. The decisive factor was that this disaster was an "Act of God" in the purest sense. When thousands are killed in an earthquake, the objection can always be raised that the houses in which the victims were trapped were not built properly, or that the people who died were living in a known earthquake zone. But the 2004 tsunami occurred literally out of the blue – there was no way any country could have been prepared for such a once-in-a-millennium event. When I spoke to a Christian friend about the disaster a few days later, he told me, apparently without irony, that "We prayed for the victims at Church on Sunday". What a pointless gesture! Either God is William Whiting's "Eternal Father, strong to save, Whose arm hath bound the restless wave…", a God who intervenes in the physical world, in which case, if benevolent, He could have diverted the wave away from populated areas or stopped it being generated in the first place, or He intervenes in people's hearts and minds, in which case He could have persuaded people to evacuate coastal areas while there was still time, or the physical laws of the universe dance their merry dance without reference to human desires or God's intervention, in which case prayer after the event was futile. But to have it all – belief in a benevolent God who can intervene but doesn't necessarily and can help people spiritually to cope with trauma they could have avoided if they had been warned in time – requires the believer to perform ultimately futile theological gymnastics of the highest order.

For anyone with eyes to see, the situation is clear – God, if He exists, is not a *personal* God who intervenes at the level of our little lives. He may be upholding the physical laws that keep the planets revolving around the stars, attracted by the gravitational pull of larger objects, and He may make water freeze at 0 degrees Celsius, and a good thing too, for if the physical laws of the universe were to shift just a fraction outside the "Goldilocks Zone" where conditions are not too hot, not too cold, but just right, then life on Earth would be impossible. Praising Him for creating and upholding the universe is therefore logical. But He is not intervening in the minutiae of our six billion lives, manipulating our brains to make us more courageous or compassionate than we would otherwise have been, making your Bible fall open at particular pages to help you make important decisions, making certain houses available for purchase or certain potential mates available for marriage. He does not change weather patterns so that you have a dry and sunny week for your Boy's Brigade camp (whatever the consequences for the farmer in the next field who is praying for rain to water his crops), He does not decide which pregnancies are going to end in miscarriage and which are going to be successful according to how deserving the potential parents are. Personal prayer, like any other form of meditation, may be useful in as much as it enables you to concentrate on a particular issue and think around it, and it may allow you to enter a trance-like state where you relax, your blood pressure is lowered and you breathe more deeply. A Catholic reciting the Hail Mary may well enter a physical and emotional state similar to that experienced by a Buddhist monk chanting or an evangelical Christian repeating a chorus. But as a way of persuading an intransigent deity to behave in certain ways, prayer does not appear to work.

What has filled the void left where a Christian faith used to be? Is G.K. Chesterton's aphorism that "When people stop believing in God, they don't believe in nothing – they believe in anything" really anything more than a clever, and rather condescending, play on words?

My initial conversion to Christianity was the result of reading a book, on that occasion the New Testament, and one of the factors in my eventual 'deconversion' was also a book, this time Richard Dawkin's "The Selfish Gene". Dawkin's work changed, if not my life, then at least my outlook on and understanding of life. An elegant theory of (almost) everything, Selfish Gene theory provides a much more satisfactory answer to questions about human behaviour (including sin, sex, racism, materialism, war) and the origins of life in general than the Bible does. Why do we often behave selfishly towards others? Because we are each programmed, at genetic level, to ensure our own survival, if necessary at the expense of others. Why do people sometimes behave in a racist or xenophobic fashion? Because they are programmed at genetic level to favour other members of their species with whom they share more genes, at the expense of those who share fewer genes. Why do we love to dress up in beautiful clothes, have our hair styled well and present an attractive face to others? Because our genes programme us to maximise our chances of mating successfully. You get the picture.

By comparison, the Bible's explanation of the origins of human behaviour, expounded in the Garden of Eden myth, has sinless Adam and Eve living in harmony with God in an earthly paradise. Satan, in the guise of a serpent, tempts Eve to eat the fruit of the Tree of Knowledge, she succumbs to his wiles, and since this ancient act of disobedience, all human beings have been sinful by their very nature ("Original Sin"). Yet what was so wrong about eating from the Tree of Knowledge? Why plant it there if its only purpose was to tempt Eve? Isn't there something vaguely sadistic about deliberately placing temptation in Adam and Eve's path just to test whether or not they would succumb? Did God want His creation to live in blissful ignorance of the world? One would had thought that He would be in favour of our obtaining knowledge.

Why create human beings with a large, energy-guzzling brain and an inquisitive nature only to rule that using that brain and satisfying that curiosity is wicked? The fact that, in orthodox Christian lore, the first sin was committed by a woman, and that it was nothing more heinous than natural curiosity, the desire to gain knowledge, speaks volumes about the Church's traditional attitudes to women and to learning. (Interestingly, because they apparently arise from completely different sources, the story of Eve eating of the Tree of Knowledge closely mirrors the Greek mythological explanation of the origin of human ills, in which Pandora is overcome with curiosity and opens the box given to her by Zeus, thus letting out into the world all the misfortunes of mankind. I would venture that both stories are attempts by misogynist men to shift responsibility for their own urges onto headstrong, rebellious women who defy the commands of a male deity).

Like every (ex-)believer before me, I have tried to construct an intellectually consistent narrative from the mass of information available, and the structure I build depends primarily on my own psychology and existing beliefs. The Gospel writers themselves, faced with a huge corpus of word-of-mouth information, hearsay and legends surrounding Jesus' life, had to filter out what they took to be untruths or exaggerations, points with which they did not agree and those they simply did not understand to create a coherent story, and each Gospel presents us with a different Jesus, reflecting the personality of the author. The differences between the Jesus of the Synoptic Gospels and the figure presented in the Gospel of John could not be greater: in Matthew's Gospel, Jesus is the fulfilment of Old Testament prophecy, a harsh, hellfire-breathing preacher; in Mark's Gospel He is the exorciser of demons.

The Synoptic Gospels in general portray Jesus in a masculine, almost aggressive light, as an archetypal alpha-male. His portrayal in John's Gospel is radically different – He is painted in softer hues, with the more 'feminine' side of his personality emphasised, and the symbols used to describe Him often relate to nurturing or to food and sustenance – living water, bread, a vine. He is the "good shepherd", the "gate for the sheep", "the way, the truth and the life".

It is interesting to reflect that, in addition to the two versions of Jesus' life that we have today (if we accept that the Jesus of the three Synoptic gospels is essentially the same character), hundreds of different Jesuses *might have been* – these versions of His story existed once but were subsequently forgotten. For every anecdote about Him, every word attributed to Him in the Gospels, hundreds of anecdotes and words once existed, lived on in the memories of those fortunate enough to have known Him but disappeared with their deaths, were passed on by word of mouth but were then forgotten, revised or pruned away over time. The fundamentalists would have us believe that the stories that survived are the true ones, and the ones that were lost or forgotten were misleading or heretical, but of course there is no way of knowing whether that is the case. What we can be sure of is that those powerful persons in the early Church who filtered the mass of information about Jesus to arrive at an orthodox version of events and orthodox quotations did so, unwittingly or not, in order to shore up their own positions, that the choice of what to leave in and what to leave out was political rather than historical.

St Paul, the real founder of Christianity and its intellectual motor, combined disparate versions of the Jesus story to create a belief system based on the sacrificial death of Christ, a reflection of the Old Testament system of animal sacrifices and the story of the first Passover in Egypt with which, as an orthodox Jew, he would have been familiar. It is unlikely that Jesus would have recognised much of Himself in the writings of Paul, which took the mass of confusing and contradictory stories about Jesus circulating around the middle of the first century AD and, many years after the event, create an ordered narrative out of relative chaos. There is certainly little in the Gospels to suggest that Jesus was aware of the supreme importance that His followers would subsequently attribute to His death.

The same process of sorting through the available information to construct a cohesive narrative and ignoring that which is contradictory or difficult to understand is undertaken by every Christian today. Kind and compassionate people create a story emphasising the love and mercy of God, to the exclusion of all the cruelty and harshness also to be found in the Bible ("The Trinity is a difficult concept to understand, but it's really all about God's love" was the opening gambit of a sermon given by the Methodist chaplain at my university one Trinity Sunday). The rightwing American Republican sees God as a divine advocate of capitalism, rewarding hard work with material riches and punishing the lazy with poverty, and finds Bible verses in support, whilst a South American liberation theologian sees God as the enemy of the rich, providing freedom for the poor and oppressed (arguably, with more scriptural justification) and offering salvation not just in the Hereafter but in the here-and-now. Those who believe in the justness of retribution for crime see God as a divine punisher of sin, a kind of celestial policeman, sacrificing Jesus on the cross to pay for our wickedness with His blood, whilst those who believe in restorative justice emphasise His infinite grace. A person's 'God story' tells you much more about them than it does about the nature of God[12]. As the writer Anne Lamott elegantly put it, "You can safely assume that you've created God in your own image when it turns out that He hates all the same people you do."

To a certain extent, I no longer have the leisure time I had back then to dwell on the abstract questions of salvation, atonement and incarnation, busy as I am with the earthier, more immediate concerns of nappy-changing, bathing and putting to bed a small child when I arrive home from work in the evenings. Collapsing into bed exhausted at a time I would once have considered ridiculous for a grown adult, I usually fall sound asleep long before my mind has turned to matters spiritual. God, the upholder of the natural world, the force behind life and the structure of the universe (if not the personal, intervening deity of the "What a friend we have in Jesus" variety) is to be found for me now in my lovely wife, my child, my wider family and the others I love, in the plants growing in my garden, the beauty of the world around me, the underlying order of the universe, rather than in any sacred writings or divine revelations. As I think of the joy in my son's face when I lift him out of his cot in the morning, how he yawns and rubs his eyes sleepily, clings to me and, if I'm especially favoured, plants a wet kiss somewhere near my ear, I'm reminded of the words of the psalmist:

The steadfast love of the Lord never ceases
His mercies never come to an end
They are new every morning
New every morning.
Great is Thy faithfulness, O Lord,
Great is Thy faithfulness[13].

---

[12] Of course, it is not just the case that different people create God in their own image, but also that the same person's God-image can change depending on their mood. My favourite example of this in the Bible in Psalm 63, attributed to David, where the psalmist starts by invoking God's love ("Your constant love is better than life itself, and so I will praise you. I will give you thanks as long as I live; I will raise my hands to you in prayer. My soul will feast and be satisfied, and I will sing glad songs of praise to you..." before, apparently without any hint of irony, cursing his enemies thus: "Those who are trying to kill me will go down into the world of the dead. They will be killed in battle, and their bodies eaten by wolves..." (spoiling an initially beautiful psalm). Is the real God to be found in the initial sentiments or the hate-filled ending of the psalm? Or is God a complex synthesis of the two? Or perhaps this psalm tells us everything about the psalmist's mental state and little about God.

[13] As adapted by Robert Davidson, ©1974, 1975 Celebration

The Great Heads and Tails Tournament

Once upon a time, a great heads and tails tournament was organised, and everyone in the world took part. The principle was easy: you turned to your nearest neighbour, threw a coin, caught it and placed it on the back of one hand, covering it with the other. Your partner called "Heads" or "Tails" and either won or lost, the winner went through to the next round, and the loser withdrew. After fewer rounds than you might imagine, everyone in the world had withdrawn, except for the final two contestants. Under the gaze of the international media, with a television audience of billions, they met, the final coin was thrown, one person won, the other lost. Amid much pomp, the winner (let's call him George) ascended the podium to be awarded the victor's crown.

When all the fuss had died down, and George was left alone to consider his victory, he started to reflect on his extraordinary story. Why should he, out of all humankind, have won the tournament? Perhaps it was because he was better than the others, somehow more equipped to correctly answer the heads-or-tails question. Perhaps he had been specially favoured, chosen by fate or the 'stars', out of all the other people in the world, to enjoy this particular honour. Or even (and this thought was so audacious that his spine tingled when he reflected on it), the whole tournament had been designed with him in mind; from the earliest stages of its planning, through its implementation to the moment when he had been proclaimed the winner, the objective had been to give him, George, the reward he so richly deserved. Yes, that was it – the tournament had been planned for his glory alone!

Poor conceited George, strutting around with his chest puffed out, acting as though he were the master of the universe. How quickly he forgot how he had reached this pinnacle — not through design or forethought, but merely through the aggregate blind, random wanderings of pure chance.

Afterword

Pascal's wager is the name of a position taken by French philosophical Blaise Pascal in his posthumously-published work *Pensées* ("Thoughts") to the question of whether or not God exists. It was a precursor of what we know nowadays as "Game Theory", a statistical discipline whereby different approaches are studied in order to maximise potential returns. Pascal postulated that, as, ultimately, we cannot know for certain about the existence or absence of a divine creator, based on the evidence around us in the natural universe, the safer bet is to assume that He *does* exist. After all, if you are a believer in this life and you turn out to be right, you will enjoy all the fruits of heaven, and if you are wrong you will have lost nothing (apart from, perhaps, the enjoyable fringe benefits of a godless life). Unbelief, on the other hand, brings no reward after death if you are right, but high costs in the form of the potential loss of salvation if you turn out to have been wrong. Therefore, merely on the basis of statistics, it is better to believe and hope for the best.

Parents who are not believers but decide to have their children baptised, "just in case...." are (in most cases unwittingly) applying Pascal's wager to their family situation, and I was tempted to apply a version of it to my own dilemma – whether to treat the writing of this book as nothing more than a cathartic exercise and leave the text to slumber unread on my hard disk, or whether to nail my colours to the mast and publish. From the evidence of the book you are holding in your hands, you can see that I decided to go ahead and publish. It feels like the end of a journey which began at a church youth meeting in 1984 and has now ended, more than twenty years later, with my arrival at a more exciting, if less certain, destination. My strong belief is that, if God exists, and in the unlikely event that He is interested in what insignificant human beings like us are up to here on Earth, He will turn out to be bigger and more broadminded than the petty, jealous little divinity portrayed by evangelical Christians. I hope that He values free-thinking, frankness and sincerity, that He loves diversity and creativity. Let us all hope that He transcends the human desire to label and categorise Him that we call "religion" and that, just as, apparently, "there will be more joy in heaven over one sinner who repents than over ninety-nine righteous persons who need no repentance" (Luke 15, verse 7) so there will be more joy over one thoughtful, enquiring person who sincerely seeks the truth, even if he ultimately gets it wrong, than over ninety-nine pious souls who accept unthinkingly whatever they are told.

Acknowledgements

I acknowledge the debt I owe to and would recommend for further reading in this area the following works:

- *The Battle for God*, by Karen Armstrong, HarperCollins, 2001

- *Big Babies*, by Michael Bywater, Granta Books, 2006

- *The Selfish Gene*, by Richard Dawkins, Oxford University Press, 2006 *(practically compulsory reading for all those who want to know where they really came from.)*

- *The God Delusion,* by Richard Dawkins, Bantam Press, 2006

- *How we know what isn't so*, by Thomas Gilovich, The Free Press, 1993

- *The Blank Slate, The Modern Denial of Human Nature*, by Stephen Pinker, Penguin Press Science, 2003

- *Rescuing the Bible from Fundamentalism: Bishop Rethinks the Meaning of Scripture,* by John Shelby Spong, HarperCollins, 2001 *(a thoughtful reflection on the absurdity of a literal interpretation of the Bible)*

- *How Mumbo-jumbo Conquered the World: A Short History of Modern Delusions*, by Francis Wheen, HarperPerennial, 2004

- *Bad Thoughts*, by Jamie Whyte, Corvo Books, 2003

and the following websites:

www.exchristian.net *(for ex-Christians, as the url implies)*

http://www.shipoffools.com *(a Christian site, refreshing for its irreverent take on the Church and lack of piety*

www.ingramcontent.com/pod-product-compliance
Lightning Source LLC
Chambersburg PA
CBHW020304290526
45784CB00003B/1350